IRON EYES CODY, THE PROUD AMERICAN

by

Iron Eyes Cody
Marietta Thompson

Empire Publishing Company, Inc.
(THE BIG REEL FOLKS)
Route 3, Box 83
Madison, NC 27025

IRON EYES CODY, THE PROUD AMERICAN

Authors: Iron Eyes Cody - Marietta Thompson

Copyright © 1988 by Empire Publishing, Inc.
Route #3, Box 83
Madison, North Carolina 27025

ISBN 0-944019-05-6 hardcover
Library of Congress Catalog Card Number 88-81378

Manufactured and printed in the United States

Other books by Empire Publishing, Incorporated:

*THE GENE AUTRY BOOK by David Rothel
*THE ROY ROGERS BOOK by David Rothel
*COWBOY SHOOTING STARS by John Rutherford and Richard B. Smith, III
*COWBOY PICTORIAL by Donald R. Key

Future books by Empire Publishing, Incorporated:

*THE LASH LaRUE BOOK
* THE ALLAN "ROCKY" LANE BOOK

CONTENTS

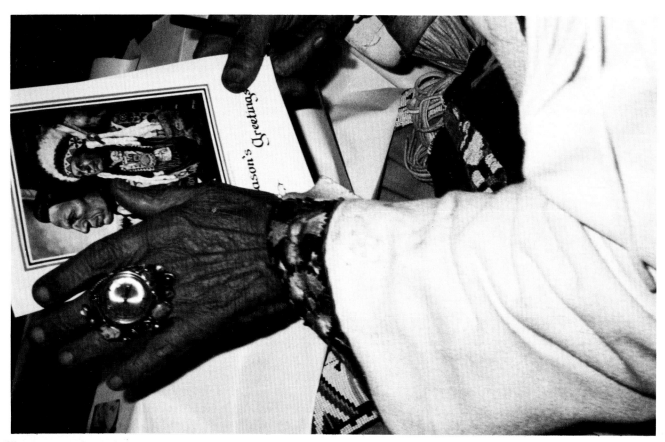

These gentle hands have signed thousands of autographs to be sold with all proceeds going to charities. Photo by Marjorie G. Freeman.

FOREWARD

Iron Eyes has in one way or another touched the lives of nearly every actor who has appeared in movies and nearly every Indian who has lived in this century. This has been through his own work beginning as a child or through his father. Iron Eyes has known all the great tribal chiefs, as well as all the great "studio chiefs" who called for him when Indian customs or lore was brought to question.

His association with heads of government -- local, state, and national -- has often placed him on the threshold of a worthwhile cause in the name of humanity. His work with "Keep America Beautiful" has led to international fame as his face is now one of the most recognized faces in the whole world. He leads a full and interesting life.

In an effort to preserve that which we want future generations to know and enjoy, we will supply photographs that will enhance, enlighten, and serve as a piece of history in itself. Scattered throughout is the handiwork of notables John Steele, Bob Timberlake, and other artist friends.

Because Iron Eyes stands for unity between the Indian and the white man, and because he lives in both worlds, it seems appropriate that both should be included in any book about him. We want to share some of our Indian heritage, some of our first American customs of which we are highly proud.

To undertake a book of any kind may require many years of collecting and planning. Research is done by drawing upon one's own knowledge and the memory and work of others. If movies are involved, much time is spent viewing as many films as possible. No one knows exactly how many movies Iron Eyes has appeared in. Our guess is over two hundred.

We have lived during a time when movies were the most exciting happening in the weekly life of each boy and girl in America. Going to "the show" on Saturday stands in our memories like the brightest light on a dark night. The anticipation of the next serial chapter, the smell of popcorn (which I popped), the congregating of friends in and around the front row (and later as teenagers on the back row), were all highlights of our young lives.

We thank you, you wonderful actors, you beautiful ladies, you handsome cowboys, you hard-working, hard-fighting Indians. Good guys and bad guys alike; we love you -- each and every one of you.

Certain portions of this book will pertain to myself, when as a child, I began a lifetime of love and respect for a certain Indian Movie Star. As my collections grew, so did my knowledge increase to the point at which Iron Eyes asked me, "Why don't you do a book?" After several years his question became, "Will you do a book with me?" To be honored in this way, my resistance could not withstand. So a beautiful working friendship combined efforts to fulfill these endeavors.

For the sake of clarity, the text will be written with the first person "I" referring to myself and the third person "he" will be Iron Eyes, except in direct quotes.

This book is a tribute to what an individual can accomplish if he sets high goals for himself and works hard. Anyone can do it. We hope it will serve as witness that one person can make a difference.
---- Marietta

INDIAN OF THE YEAR 1984

IRON EYES CODY • CHEROKEE CREE

J. STEELE ©

DEDICATION
BY IRON EYES

This book is dedicated to my grandson, Iron Chebon, who will carry forth the ways of tradition; to my granddaughters, Teressa and Raven; and to the memory of my dear wife, Birdie.

DEDICATION
BY MARIETTA

This book is dedicated to my husband, Ed, for his patience; to my son, Rickey, who says, "Mom, you can do it;" to all of you with Indian heritage, both real and reel; to you film buffs everywhere who have fond memories of playing Cowboys and Indians.

ABOUT THE PUBLISHER

In the spring of 1974, Empire Publishing Company came into existence when it began publishing a newspaper for movie collectors entitled The BIG REEL which has since become a 100+ page monthly tabloid publication read by movie buffs worldwide. Movie collectors everywhere exclaim that The BIG REEL is the very best source to buy, trade, and sell movie-related material.

Donald and Noreen Key, creators and founders of The BIG REEL, retain ownership and remain very active at Empire Publishing Company with the capable assistance of Evon Walker and Rhonda Lemons. Each month, the tabloid is chocked full of advertisements from individual collectors, nostalgia dealers, and others who have a desire to contact collectors with similar hobby interests. The BIG REEL also contains special articles, feature stories, obituaries of movie-related persons, nostalgic photos, book and video reviews, and many items of interest for movie and television collectors.

July 1987 was another milestone date for Empire Publishing Company, as it entered the book-publishing business with its release of the never-before-offered ROY ROGERS BOOK, written by nationally-known western movie authority David Rothel. Since that date, another book by David Rothel, The GENE AUTRY BOOK, has been published by Empire. Both of these books are available for sale from the publisher.

The latest book published by Empire is a very helpful reference book entitled COWBOY SHOOTING STARS which is authored by John A. Rutherford and Richard B. Smith, III. Within its pages, the B-western movie buff can find all the cowboy stars' names, a complete listing of the B-western films each made, the year each title was released, the studio which released each film, and the running time of each film.

Other books in the making which will be offered in the near future by Empire Publishing Company include publications on the movie careers of the "King of the Bullwhip," Lash LaRue and Allan "Rocky" Lane.

You are now holding in your hands the latest Empire Publishing release, IRON EYES CODY, THE PROUD AMERICAN. We trust you will enjoy learning about the life and times of this great American Indian through the words and many pictures within these pages.

Now, there are two proud Americans --- one, of course, being Iron Eyes Cody, the Keep America Beautiful, tear in his eye proud American; and the other being all of us at Empire Publishing Company for having been given the opportunity and privilege of publishing this book about the great American, Iron Eyes Cody. He has given so much of himself to others; Iron Eyes Cody truly loves his country and his fellowman, and he strives daily to make this world a better place in which for us to live.

All books may be ordered directly from the publisher - Empire Publishing, Inc.
Route #3, Box 83
Madison, N.C. 27025

ACKNOWLEDGMENTS

A picture book would have been zero, nothing, without the photos that we hold so dear in our longtime collections and for which we express our gratitude to Keep America Beautiful, Inc., to the many studios for the lobby cards, stills and posters. To you photographers who so graciously contributed over the years to the personal picture history with notations on back of photos "Please give credit," this is for you. You are wonderful. Thank you. The credit is yours.

Jack Oakman, Clarksdale, MS., thank you for invaluable help on the film listing.

For the paintings, drawings, etc. our appreciation goes to John Steele, Bob Timberlake and to the memory of Clarence Ellsworth. Special thanks to Richard R. Tworg for the cover photo.

To Colleen Colson, Tom Constantino, Joe and Marie Levy, A. C. Lyles, Maurice McGehee, Van Smith, Polly Stoner, and Wilma Strough, who assisted in a variety of ways, you are indispensable friends.

10

SPECIAL
ACKNOWLEDGMENT

The Great Spirit Prayer that Iron Eyes gives to open all the meetings is requested of him wherever he goes. It is a beautiful prayer that transcends race and creed; and Iron Eyes delivers it graciously in words and sign language, or sometimes uses the symbolic peace pipe.

When this prayer is completed, most people applaud because the world would be a better place if we all lived by its words.

It is with honor and pride as we begin this labor of love, to draw from our Indian heritage:

THE GREAT SPIRIT PRAYER

Oh Great Spirit whose voice in the winds I hear,
And Whose Breath gives life to all the world –
Hear me.
Before You I come, one of Your many children.
Small and weak am I.
Your strength and wisdom I need.
Make me walk in beauty.
Make my heart respect all you have made.
My ears to hear Your Voice.
Make me wise that I may know all You have taught
    my people.
The lessons You have hidden in every rock.
I seek strength, not to be superior to my brother.
Make me able to fight my greatest enemy – myself.
Make me ready to stand before You with clean and
    straight eyes.
When life fades, as the fading sunset, may our
    spirits stand before You without shame.

Recently in Los Angeles, I was pleased to present to Iron Eyes a handmade needle-point tapestry of The Great Spirit Prayer. The 18x28 inch wall hanging contains eighty-nine thousand stitches, over one thousand yards of yarn, and required four hundred ninety-two hours to complete.

I was honored when Johnny Crawford (Mark of Rifleman-TV fame) asked if I would make one for sale; but I never make a needlepoint for sale, just as a gift to a very special person.

Now a second honor has come. Iron Eyes has notified me that the above tapestry has been selected by the curators as an addition to Gene Autry's Western Heritage Museum.

INTRODUCING
MARIETTA THOMPSON

Many of you already know Marietta; but for those of you who do not, I want you to meet my co-author. She is a member of the Native American Indian Association of Tennessee. Marietta is part Cherokee, part Choctaw, and part Lumbee. She is Baptist. She lives with her wonderful family on a farm near Tuckerman, Arkansas. Marietta is a great lady!

When she agreed to be my co-author, I knew the book I'd been wanting to do would finally become a reality. She knows many of my Star friends, some through her work with the Membership Committee of the Memphis (Tennessee) Film Festival; others I've introduced her to when she visits with me.

She assists me at powwows and other activities; my Indian friends love her. She helps raise money for the Indian Centers, for the Hope Ranch for children, and helps me sell my autographs. She makes copies of The Great Spirit Prayer to give to lots of people; many requests come to her through the mail for these prayers.

For many years she worked with the Social Services in Arkansas, with the blind, the handicapped, the senior citizens and the children. Out of her car she operated a clothing bank for anyone needing clothing.

She was a Charter Member and First Elected President of the Tuckerman, Arkansas, Jaycee Auxiliary. She had two articles published in the Arkansas Jaycee Magazine: one was serious, and the other was a fun thing about needing a bath. She's a hard worker and even helped to physically build a park. I was pleased to present her with my Iron Eyes Cody Peace Medal in the name of brotherhood, unity, and friendship.

Marietta has been my Number One Fan since she was about ten years old. She had to ask the theater manager my name; then a lifetime of collecting began. In order to

Ben Johnson, Marietta, and Iron Eyes, 1987

earn her spending money at age thirteen, she got her first job at her home town theater in Fisher, Arkansas. She was watching as the electric popcorn popper shocked the girl who operated it. She was there when the girl quit and walked out. She ran, asked for the job, and got it. On the concrete floor she put wooden Coca Cola cases upside down to stand on; that stopped most of the shocks. And she got to see the movies for free. When the manager learned that she was making all A's in school, he asked her to sell tickets. Up the ladder she went.

Her love of the movies, those great westerns, deepened. She filled scrapbooks with her collections. She has been writing to me for many, many years, sending me things that I like. I think she knows more about my career than I know myself. I have many friends; but two that I rate right up there at the top are Ben Johnson and Marietta Thompson.

With officiating Master of Ceremonies, Sammy "Tonekei" White, on October 18, 1987, at Mt. Juliet, Tennessee Inter-tribal Powwow, in traditional ceremony, I officially adopted Marietta as my daughter, presented her to the tribes before a thousand people, and bestowed upon her the Cherokee name "Oxshinnia" (You Are The One).

----Iron Eyes Cody

Cowboys have been known to kiss their horses; well, Indians love their horses, too. Iron Eyes with Pecos Pete: More than a pet, a treasured friend.

CHAPTER 1
HOLLYWOOD CAREER

"I'm a Star only when I'm working. When I go home, I'm just me, Iron Eyes."

The career of Iron Eyes in Hollywood may have been predestined by his grandfather, Randolph Abshire Codey. He had nothing to do with films, but during the Civil War, he was a member of Quantrill's Raiders, and spent two years in jail for his crimes of theft. Upon release, Randolph Abshire Codey decided to alter, somewhat, his way of making a living. He started a legitimate ranch with some horses he had previously stolen. As fathers do, he taught the business to his son, Thomas Longplume.

Longplume developed his own manner of larceny in stealing horses. He knew so much about animals that it was easy for him to set up a phoney veterinarian service to fool people by making horses appear to be in worse shape than they were, buy them for the low "glue-factory" price, then patch them up properly, and sell those fine animals for a high profit.

As an expert with the bow and arrow, ropes and bullwhips, and trick riding, Longplume, along with old Sitting Bull himself, traveled with Buffalo Bill's Wild West Show in season. Everywhere they went he gathered Indian artifacts, met different tribes, and became an authority on Indian languages, sign language, and tribal customs. He and his wife, Frances, made most of the costumes used in the shows. Longplume even changed the spelling of the family name to "Cody" to be more like Buffalo Bill Cody.

Longplume had a special way with the stories he told of Buffalo Bill and the Indians that would leave people wanting to hear more. He was often asked to lecture and was good at it, but there wasn't much money in that.

On the night of April 3, 1912, Iron Eyes was born near Fort Gibson, Oklahoma. The location is not definite because his mother, Frances Salpit Cody of the Cree Tribe, was outside somewhere, hiding from Iron Eyes' abusive father who was drunk and in a rage.

The year is also questionable. His birthdate has been listed anywhere from 1907 to 1915, because his age was changed by his father to cover any particular need at a particular time, making him younger or older for the purpose of show business. Iron Eyes once went to Europe on his older brother's passport.

He recalls that when he was 13, his dad was technical advisor for Howard Hughes. One morning Longplume was

Thomas Longplume Cody, 1904

Frances Salpit Cody, 1909

16

drunk and Iron Eyes told Howard he could do his father's work. "Your father said you are just ten years old," remarked Howard. "But I'm thirteen, not ten," replied Iron Eyes. He got the job.

Iron Eyes knows that he was 14 when he and Birdie met during the making of the silent film THE SCARLET LETTER. Because it was made in 1926, we arrived at 1912 as his birthdate.

From the age of three, Iron Eyes, then called Oscar "Little Eagle," could already repeat The Great Spirit Prayer. The young Indian also knew some sign language and rope tricks, and he was allowed to accompany Longplume with the wild west shows. When Iron Eyes became school age, his mother saw to it that he went to school; but he had rather have been out riding horses.

Iron Eyes never missed anything that was going on at the ranch and was under foot when some representatives of Famous Players Lasky (later Paramount) dropped by for a visit. They had learned that Longplume owned a ranch with a corn field that they needed for a movie they were making - BACK TO GOD'S COUNTRY. They knew also that the other Indians of the area would follow his lead to work for them.

Iron recalls that first glimpse of movie making as a Civil War picture with some prisoners escaping from camp. In it, five little Indians, including himself, played in the corn field, backed up against buildings, kid-type things.

At one point someone noticed how daresome Iron Eyes was, and asked Longplume to let him do a bit more. Iron Eyes stood by a corral gate and let a horse jump over him, proving his bravery then and there.

From his Cherokee father, Iron Eyes learned bravery, a knowledge of animals, and a real concern for the well-being of the Indian people as a whole.

Longplume liked the looks of the movie money, a crisp, new, hundred dollar bill. Because people were beginning to catch on to his horse "doctoring," it was a good time to leave Oklahoma. So thanks to Grandfather Randolph's legacy of larceny, the move was necessary, and California seemed the best place.

The century was still young. Most roads were not paved. There was radio, but no TV. Movies were just getting started, with inventions and changes yet to take place. Lighting had not been perfected, so the sun was utilized. Sets were built in front of the camera. And the camera didn't move until the sun did. Movies were silent. No need for "quiet on the set" back then.

Longplume was already familiar with Hollywood because he had been there between wild west shows and had done some small scale advising and bit parts in the movies. Iron Eyes had hoped that with the move, his father would give up drinking, but he didn't. Soon afterward, his parents were divorced. His mother married a man named Dillian and stayed with him until his death, after which she and Longplume got back together.

Frances Salpit's children in order of birth were: Emery Cody, Joseph W. "Silvermoon" Cody, Oscar "Little Eagle" (Iron Eyes) Cody, Frank "Red Star" Dillian, Harry Dillian, Victoria "White Bird" Dillian. There were also three adopted: Nolan Abshire, Laura Abshire, and Mae Abshire.

The family business of renting out Indian props and costumes was going good. Silvermoon hired the Indians and Longplume did the technical directing for various producers, taught sign language and how to make smoke signals.

More and more however, Longplume would be too drunk to satisfy his obligations and Iron Eyes would fill in for him, as for the movie FIGHTING BLOOD in 1921. Longplume received the credit and and the pay for Iron Eyes' work; but before long, directors and producers began to realize what was going on, just how much Iron Eyes was doing, and how well he did it. He was then accepted as a very young and knowledgeable technical advisor in his own right.

Most of the time the Codys were losing the battle of trying to get producers to do Indian things in a realistic way. Longplume did try, but the need to earn a living came first. Iron Eyes planned for the day when he would carry enough weight to see it done correctly.

THE COVERED WAGON movie epic

Okies from Oklahoma. The three Cody Brothers, left to right, Iron Eyes, Silvermoon, and Red Star, in a publicity photo for TREACHERY RIDES THE RANGE, Warner Brothers, 1936.

came along in 1923, starring Mary Miles Minter. Longplume and Silvermoon were both in the Indian scenes. Iron Eyes, while not in the movie, was one of a group of Indian kids who danced and put on a live prologue at the theater before the movie began; he did the same kind of advertising for THE IRON HORSE in 1924, which starred George O'Brien.

Beginning with THE COVERED WAGON, a man who played an important role in bringing realistic interpretations of Indians to the screen was Colonel Tim McCoy. Tim, along with the Cody family, was responsible for assembling and training 500 Arapaho, Cheyenne, and Sioux.

Dressed in feathers and full ceremonial garb, just like the Indians, Tim entered a dance competition at the Cody Stampede of 1921, and won first place against the best Sioux dancer, Chief Red Wolf. Longplume and Iron Eyes saw the whole thing.

Tim's proficiency in sign language and Indian dialects led to his adoption by the Arapahoes who named him "High Eagle."

After THE COVERED WAGON, Tim gathered the more striking Indian personalities, including Longplume and Iron Eyes, and took the troop into several Eastern theaters and toured Europe with them.

Longplume's early movie appearances included: THE BIRTH OF A NATION (1915), THE LAST OF THE DUANES (1919), THE COVERED WAGON (1923), THE IRON HORSE and NORTH OF 36 (1924).

His oldest brother Emery was out and gone most of the time, so Iron Eyes really didn't know him very well. It was Silvermoon whom Iron Eyes followed after and to whom he was closest.

Silvermoon had a strong, muscular body which led to his being chosen as an advertising model for Bonomo Body Building that claimed to be a scientific physical culture course that would build a he-man body in ninety days (or money back?). He didn't need the course, but it didn't hurt him any; and it did get his picture in the periodicals, showing his physique.

Silvermoon was an expert in archery, a fine horseman with ropes. It was he who taught Gene Autry the artistry of the bullwhip.

Frank "Red Star" Dillian was also known as "Cody" because he came to Hollywood to be with Iron Eyes and was in a few movies. He, Silvermoon, and Iron Eyes did work together in one movie, TREACHERY RIDES THE RANGE, 1936.

Red Star was known as the intelligent one in the family. He completed his college education (Iron Eyes quit after two years), and could finish a crossword puzzle quicker than any of his friends. It was while hanging around a movie set, working a puzzle, that he was noticed by an executive of Broadway Department Store, who offered him the head clerk position. Red Star didn't care much for acting anyway.

He married a blonde, Swedish Woman named Freda. The memory of that wedding stands out because the minister, who was drunk, nearly married Freda to Iron Eyes by mistake. Red Star died after being hit by a car one evening as he was leaving the store.

Half-brother, Harry Dillian had diabetes and when he learned he didn't have long to live, he jumped out of a car and killed himself.

Half-sister, Victoria "White Bird" Dillian ran an all Indian store. She married Chief Yowlachie who thrilled us in numerous movies. Yes, Yowlachie was Iron Eyes' brother-in-law.

Some famous people entered the family through the marriage of Iron Eyes to Bertha "Ga Yewas" Darkcloud Parker. Her father, Dr. Arthur C. Parker, a noted archaeologist, ethnologist, writer, speaker, editor, founded National Indian Day in 1914. Libraries still house many of the superb books he wrote on the Iroquois. In 1925, Parker was appointed Director of the Rochester Museum in New York; some of his fine collection of Seneca jewelry is on display there in memory of his daughter, Bertha, who was affectionately known as "Birdie."

The first Indian to become a U.S. Commissioner of Indian Affairs was General Ely S. Parker, a great, great uncle of Birdie. He knew Grant, Lee, and all the notables of Civil War days.

Birdie was truly from an impressive family, the Turtle Clan of The Seneca Tribe. She impressed Iron Eyes, too, with a great smile. She was thin and shapely;

Silvermoon Cody coaching Gene Autry in the use of the whip.

and he knew from the moment he laid eyes on her that she was the one for him. They met while working in the movie THE SCARLET LETTER, 1926. She was an extra; Silvermoon and Iron Eyes were "roach-head" Indians with shaved heads. M.G.M. had to keep them under contract until the hair grew back out so they got more work that way.

Iron Eyes told Birdie that he was going to marry her; but she had her own ideas on that. Her Indian name meant "elusive," and it took Iron Eyes two years to convince her to marry him "the Indian way," after which they just "went steady" until they were older and were married by a Justice of the Peace.

It wasn't surprising that Birdie possessed the same scientific qualities as her father. She loved to go on field trips but she wouldn't dig in any burial grounds. Her uncle, Dr. Harrington, Curator of the Southwest Museum, Los Angeles, took her

to Nevada on one such trip in 1930. Her dog went down into a cave and began to bark. Upon investigation, Birdie found a giant sloth skull, and received worthwhile publicity, earning her title "scientist."

The Southwest Museum, where she had been working at everything from telephone operator to caretaker, promoted her to Assistant in Archaeology. For the rest of her life she devoted as much time as possible to making that museum the very best in every respect. She was a brilliant writer and contributed regularly to THE MASTERKEY, the museum publication of technical data on Indian art, crafts, gems and ways of life.

Birdie made beautifully detailed beadwork, some of which Iron Eyes continues to wear. She did the beadwork for the movie TULSA (1949), and appeared in several movies herself. In between all that hard work, she gave Iron Eyes three children: Wilma, Robert and Arthur.

Birdie with daughter, Wilma

Wilma died tragically in a hunting accident while visiting her grandmother. Robert and Arthur grew up in a traditional Indian home, became skilled in the art of intricate dance, and both are Eagle Scouts.

Robert married a descendant of Chief Joseph of the Nez Perce. They have two children on the Umitilla Reservation in Oregon.

Arthur is a staff sergeant in the Marines. He married a lady from the Philippine Islands, and they have one child.

And now back to the movies ---. Similarities often happen in the making of movies. For instance, Iron Eyes was in both versions of THE SCARLET LETTER: the first was 1926 silent (Lillian Gish); the second was 1934 talkie with Colleen Moore.

He was in two versions of ROSE MARIE: 1927 with Joan Crawford and 1935 with Jeanette McDonald and Nelson Eddy. He furnished props and costumes for both of these as well as for the 1951 movie THE WILD NORTH which was based on ROSE MARIE, and for the 1954, third making of ROSE MARIE.

The Indian dancing in all the ROSE MARIE related movies was accomplished through Iron Eyes' teaching.

In addition to making movies, costumes, and going to school, Iron Eyes spent some of his time in outdoor theater work. He was in excellent physical condition as a sixteen-mile runner and could keep up on foot with others on horses.

Iron Eyes' stage appearances include: THE AMERICAN, 1930; MY BLOSSOM BRIDE, 1931; and WHITE GOD AND RED GOD, 1932.

With the advent of "talkies," picture shows became America's number one pastime. In a movie theater a person could dream and lose himself for a couple of hours; and if time permitted, one could sit through the second showing, at no charge, to see if something of interest could possibly happen the same way twice.

Often the character name was remembered ahead of the actors whose names we didn't know. We did a lot of "face recognizing." It was helpful when some studios would, at the beginning or end of a picture, show the actor, his name, and his character name.

When credits were run, sometimes he wasn't called at all; but if I looked for him, I would see him; and if I listened, I would hear him. Nobody could yell like Iron Eyes. His war whoop was a cinematic trademark. And if the arrow hit its mark, even though it might not be shown who shot it, I would surmise from whence it came.

If Iron Eyes rode with the front row of Indians, I knew he was apt to have a speaking part; but if he rode with the second row and did not speak, I still thought I could hear him whispering directions to the others. His face told me he was keeping an eye on them; he was the leader. His presence enhanced each of his films.

The path to stardom has been paved for many actors by veteran stuntmen such as Yakima Canutt and Jock O'Mahoney. Stuntman Neil Summers, who for three seasons worked on THE FALL GUY, TV series, can tell hilarious stories about incidents that have happened to him. It takes

Indian family all dressed up. Robert, Arthur, Birdie, and Iron Eyes.

careful planning and know-how to perform difficult feats successfully.

Actors who are in good physical condition often want to try their own stunts, maybe to prove fitness, but usually early in a career, it is to pad the pocketbook.

Certainly an Indian would like to prove his prowess, but just consider that Iron Eyes could earn an extra five dollars each time he took a fall. Well, for the money he would fall off horses all day! Then over the years, the price rose to ten, twenty, fifty, and a hundred dollars; but by the time the price got better, producers required him to use a double.

During the filming of THEY DIED WITH THEIR BOOTS ON (1941), Iron Eyes was accidentally shot in the back by Errol Flynn with a blank at close range. He

22

was lying on the ground in desperate pain, bleeding, and couldn't move. The action continued until the scene was finished; and when the director came over to compliment him on the excellent stunt, they found him passed out.

At other times bones have been broken. Once a horse fell on Iron Eyes and smashed him. Those who get hurt, make up for the physical losses with a strong will to continue.

Robert Cody, Iron's son, doubled for him in LIGHT IN THE FOREST (Disney, 1958); but it was the great Al Wyatt who generally performed as his double. On occasion a dummy was used, but only handsome dummies qualified.

Iron Eyes did some adventure films in which he did not play an Indian, and nationally was not a prerequisite, such as a deck hand in THE SEA WOLF (1941). However, his philosophy is that Indians should play Indians. They make fairly good Mexicans and the like, but as Indians they are top-notch.

An Indian can spend long periods of time on a horse, in the blazing hot sun, and they already look like Indians. White men make silly-looking Indians, unrealistic. I've often wondered why producers didn't use real Indians who needed the work.

Producers did things wrong for so long that maybe they couldn't recognize what was right. They made all Indians look like Apaches. To dress a Sioux like an Apache could start a war in itself. Most tribes didn't wear war bonnets, but in the movies the more war bonnets, the better the film makers liked it. Iron Eyes kept insisting that each tribe should be properly dressed.

From the way Indians were represented in movies, one would have thought the only word they knew was "UGH." It's no wonder audiences thought Indians were lunatics, especially if they knew no Indians.

Well, I met a real Indian, Iron Eyes Cody! And believe me, he didn't say "ugh" even once. He did wear braids and a feather, a style that he copied from his father that has now become another trademark. I was honored to be in his presence.

The first movie that most of us re-

member in which the audience took the Indians' side was BROKEN ARROW (1949); in it Indians were a proud dignified race of warriors with their own code of honor, culture, and justifiable hatred of the white man. The Association on American Indian Affairs gave it a special award.

Even though there are 499 Federally recognized tribes and groups, including 218 Native Alaskan Communities, Indian people are one of the smallest of minorities and have extremely hard times. Racial prejudice and the widespread feeling that Indians are quaint, strange, and brutally savage, has been fed by the motion picture industry. This has added to the obstacles that Indians are trying to overcome.

For instance, all Indians are not drunks. Women resent being called "squaw." A young man is a "brave," not a "buck."

Most people agree that the main culprit of the stereotyped Indian (looking in a broken piece of a mirror, holding a handful of beads, throwing a tomahawk, stealing firewater) has been the media, movies. Iron Eyes' own son asked him if he had ever scalped anyone. That provoked an even stronger desire for truth in film.

Always at odds with producers, Iron Eyes is an ageless picture of integrity, piercing sincerity, straightforwardness. He radiates honesty and can be depended upon to do the right thing. Aren't we of Indian heritage grateful that Iron Eyes is there to push for realism in film?

An old newspaper clipping in my collection about the making of ANNIE GET YOUR GUN in 1950, quotes Keenan Wynn telling about the featured Cherokee Indian, Iron Eyes Cody, who supplied the Indian costumes, etc. He said, "Iron Eyes hired a van, drove it to the outskirts of Griffith Park where his Moosehead Museum stands, loaded the van with beaded mocassins, suede hunting jackets, war bonnets, etc., and put a sign on the museum door, "CLOSED UNTIL I FINISH PLAYING INDIAN."

I've wondered many times why American Indians are called "red men" when in fact, some are ivory, some are copper, and some are quite dark. If a white man were sun burned or wind burned, he'd be redder than an Indian.

It was believed that Indians in battle scenes could get killed several times in a movie and no one would notice. Iron Eyes would get shot, fall off a horse, get trampled, get up and do it all over again. Who would know the difference? In 1948 when I was ten years old and already an avid fan of Iron Eyes, I saw him get knifed and killed in C. B. DeMille's THE UNCONQUERED and later resurrected with a shaved head, carrying a hot spear, torturing a frantic Paulette Goddard. Did Iron Eyes really believe it wouldn't be noticed? In a few days he got a letter from me to that effect. To this day, he remembers that letter.

Being a First American technical advisor requires one to have a knowledge of famous Indians. Many famous Indians hold a place of greatness in the history of the United States. Some were warriors: Geronimo, Crazy Horse, Pontiac, and Osceola; they showed their bravery against the white man and earned a much deserved respect for their courage.

We remember the poem "Hiawatha" by Henry Wadsworth Longfellow, and how many know that Hiawatha was a statesman who formed the great Iroquois League?

There was Sequoya who believed in peaceful adjustment to the new ways; Samoset and Massosoit were the Indians who helped the pilgrims survive the difficult years in New England. When Lewis and Clark were seeking the Pacific Ocean, it was Sacagawea who guided them so successfully.

Sitting Bull, the famous Medicine Man of the Hunkpapa Teton Sioux, was an artist who sketched his battles with the Crow. Some of his work is housed in the Smithsonian Institute.

A good director does research and studies continually in his efforts for realism. An Indian director has to keep in mind that each tribe aspires to protect and preserve its own identity.

Often scripts came from those who had no first hand experience; therefore, imagination was mixed with the truth. The reel west was fabricated with the real west.

Western movies contained certain standardized themes that were used over and over: building a railroad, a wagon train, an Indian attack, gold strike, bank holdup, run-away wagon with a pretty girl inside, a cattle or buffalo stampede, saloon fight, and pony express, to name a few. Intertwined there might be a campfire, singing cowboys, crooked gamblers, dance hall girls, house raisings, barn burnings, a poison sign after a thirst had been quinched, and the good guys in white hats riding off into the sunset.

With good triumphant over evil, western movies accomplished all they were meant to be. They provided the best, most enduring, most endearing entertainment we could have wanted. The memory of Saturday night's movie would linger all week. We survived on them; they brought us through. And weren't they fun?

Remember the spellbinding serials? Especially those of Republic which had great music that provided excitement to whatever was happening. If all else failed, the music made the chapter.

Of the many radio shows that Iron Eyes has appeared on, it was THE LONE INDIAN on KFBW in Los Angeles during the thirties that is most vivid in his memory. It featured Iron Eyes, his wife, Birdie, and Uncle Big Tree, traveling around the country with a white man in a covered wagon.

Each place they stopped to camp or rest was the setting of a lesson in history of a particular tribe of the area. Iron Eyes portrayed all the great chiefs in the travels.

One day Big Tree was too drunk to read, and at the last minute, a musical group was found to substitute for them: The Rocky Mountaineers who had just hired a new vocalist named Leonard Slye (later Roy Rogers). The announcer surprised them by introducing them on the air as The Sons of the Pioneers. The name stuck. And a great friendship began for Iron Eyes and Roy Rogers.

Most people knew very little about television until 1948 or thereabouts. As it became popular, we wondered how much effect it would have in the lives of movie stars. One star who accepted and faired well by it was the multi-talented Iron Eyes Cody. He began in the late forties to sandwich TV shows in between his main meal of movies. California youngsters

With Tim McCoy. "Was Tae" (good).

were thrilled at THE TIM McCOY AND IRON EYES SHOW on KTLA. Sometimes it was called TIM McCOY AND HIS PAL IRON EYES. They began each program by saying "Was Tae" (sounds like "Wash Day") and giving the sign for its meaning "good." They told stories about The West.

When Tim left the show, Iron Eyes and Birdie put together their own program of legends, customs, crafts, and dances, called IRON EYES ADVENTURE. They set up a tepee, dressed themselves and their two sons in authentic costumes, and let people have a glimpse of real Indian life. I have a tape of a couple of those shows; and let me say that two-year-old Robert could really dance in the double trailer war bonnet that proud father made for him. Today that little war bonnet is the property of Iron Chebon Cody, Robert's son, on the Umitilla Reservation in Oregon.

As television really took off, more and more offers came Iron Eyes' way. Guest spots include: Marcus Welby, Medi-cal Center, Governor & J.J., Cimarron Strip, Death Valley Days, Destry, Desi-Lucy Show, Daniel Boone, The FBI, George Goble Show, The Immortal, Lawman, Mc-Millan and Wife, Maverick, Mr. Ed, Phil Harris Show, The Pioneers, Rawhide, The Rebel, Sgt. Preston, Then Came Bronson, The Tall Man, Wild Bill Hickok, Wyatt Earp, Zane Grey Theatre, Warpath, Gun-slinger, Newhart, and the Danny Thomas Show.

Twice Iron Eyes was on The MIKE DOUGLAS SHOW. Mike told him to cut The Great Spirit Prayer short. Iron Eyes said, "I can do it in one minute," and pro-ceeded to show him. That is the shorten-ed version as it remains today.

He stumped the panel on WHAT'S MY LINE with his book, INDIAN TALK.

As of late, Manitou Productions of Ontario, Canada, persuaded Iron Eyes to do a series, THE WILDERNESS TRAIL, in the role of The Shaman.

FANTASY ISLAND with Ricardo

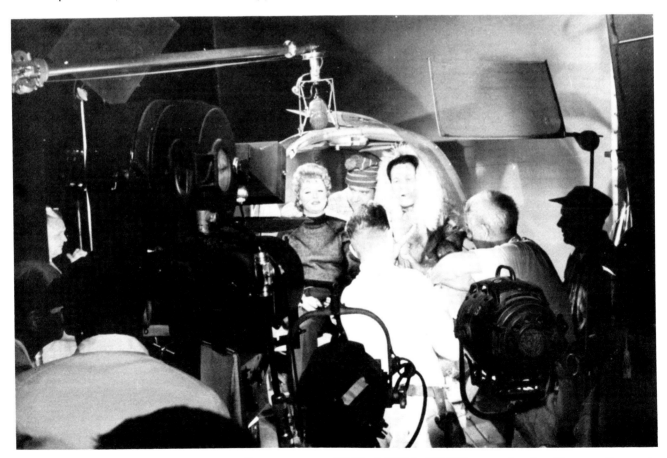

Lucille Ball and Iron Eyes in helicopter on THE LUCY SHOW: episode "Lucy Goes to Alaska."

Montalban, Herve Villechaize, and Mary Ann Mobley, allowed him a good part as an old spirit.

Herb Larsen's OFF HAND program on the Silent Network presented Iron Eyes comparing the American Indian sign language with the American sign language.

Requests for advertisements have come on a regular basis. Some that come to mind are: American Petroleum Institute (1959) and TWA (1968). Twice he and Sunset Carson (movie cowboy and rodeo star) made commercials for United Airlines with Iron Eyes asking Sunset, "Does this mean I'm your favorite Indian?" To which Sunset would reply, "No, Ghandi was." During the last take, Sunset as a joke switched his answer to, "No, Tonto was." That surprised Iron Eyes and he smiled. United kept both versions.

Iron Eyes says, "There is no way to name all the department stores, hardware stores, and hamburger joints I have helped to open."

According to historian Iron Eyes, Hollywood was born February 1, 1887. A fellow from Kansas named Harvey Wilcox started it all when he subdivided and started selling the one hundred twenty acres he owned in Southern California.

The town incorporated in 1903 with a population figure of 700. In 1910, Hollywood was annexed and became a district of Los Angeles in order to have water and sewer. Population had grown to five thousand in just seven years.

The famous Hollywood sign on Mount Lee originally was Hollywoodland, an advertisement for the subdivision. The

1980 Commercial for Rustler's Steak House

letters were fifty feet high and thirty feet wide. The last four letters were removed in 1945, and the word, as we know it best, was left for posterity.

A new sign was constructed in 1978 at a cost of a quarter of a million dollars. The lucky people who received a piece of the original sign claim to have the rarest of treasures. In general the sign has served as a symbol of all our dreams.

Iron Eyes still frequents the famous Musso & Frank Grill which opened in 1919 on Hollywood Boulevard. They serve great steaks! He honored me by asking me to lunch with him there. We sat in one of the booths with Alan Hale, Jr. (Skipper on GILLIGANS' ISLAND, TV) who had just finished his meal. Then before we were finished, Johnny Crawford (Mark on RIFLEMAN, TV) and his wife came over to say hello. As we were leaving, Iron Eyes pointed out the booths that his various star friends used to claim daily.

What about Hollywood and Vine that was once the crossroads of all movieland? Iron Eyes took me there to answer all my questions. The location today contains no awareness of moviedom. It houses a restaurant, an office building, a travel agency, and a vacant store. However, as long as I live, the corner of "Hollywood and Vine" will hold a place in my heart. And I have been there!

With a twinkle in his eye, Iron Eyes calls Hollywood "A Celebrity Zoo;" but he loves it. He is a part of that zoo and we

1971 Xerox commercial

are glad he is.

California continues to be the leading state in population – 26,900,000 in 1987. I guess it proves that California still holds that certain magic.

When questioned as to which movies about Indians meet with his approval, in a realistic sense, Iron Eyes answered, "BROKEN ARROW, A MAN CALLED HORSE, GRAYEAGLE, LITTLE BIG MAN, and WINTERHAWK."

I personally believe that in GRAY-EAGLE (1977), perfection is personified in the charismatic combination of Ben Johnson, Jack Elam, Lana Wood, Alex Cord and Iron Eyes.

To the list of great Indians, I would like to add the name of Iron Eyes Cody whom I believe is the greatest Indian, the most gentle, caring humanitarian to live in the 20th Century. He really should have been a chief. He would have been a great one!

He has brought truth, realism, and understanding to western movies and to the modern people who make those films. Iron Eyes deserves a standing ovation from western movie lovers everywhere!

The cowboys, Indians, and friends are the finest people on earth in the use of excuses as reasons to get together, visit, and reminisce. Western reunions are probably more fun than any other kind, with the casual western dress, blue jeans, boots, hats, (or war bonnets), etc.

Many is the time that Iron Eyes has been lassoed by the cowboys and cowgirls to help celebrate an auspicious occasion, an anniversary, or a charitable cause. He treasures friendships and is glad to lend a helping hand or join in personal celebrations.

One of the greatest western reunions took place in October, 1981, in Nashville, Tennessee, as THE NASHVILLE PALACE honored Roy Rogers' 50th year in show

The painting of famous stars to which Iron Eyes is pointing, covers an outside wall of a building in Hollywood. Iron Eyes furnished the paint for the artist to use.

business. The television program aired on NBC, November 7, 1981.

When I want to meet the Stars, I plan ahead by watching for announcements of charity fund raisers that Stars support, buy a ticket to the dinner, and participate where the stars gather.

One such fund raiser that is of particular interest to western film fans is The Golden Boot Awards, a looked-for-ward-to annual reunion, held in Los Angeles to benefit The Motion Picture and Television Country House and Hospital.

Usually held in August, the $150.00 per person ticket includes a delicious evening meal and entertainment with Stars such as Gene Autry, Roy Rogers, Dale Evans, Fess Parker, George Montgomery, Clayton Moore, Bob Steele, Monte Hale, Ben Johnson, Lee Majors, Sunset Carson, James Arness, Chuck Connors, Amanda Blake, the likes of which most people have never seen before in one place.

Iron Eyes is a real part of this festivity; among other things, he opens the program with The Great Spirit Prayer.

Possibly a dozen or more Stars, including writers, musicians, etc., will receive awards, and just as many will be presenters. Considering that many of today's Stars are fans themselves of the Western Stars, there's no way to guess who will be at which table. It is the best one hundred and fifty dollars a person can

This is my prized possession – THE NASHVILLE PALACE, ROY ROGERS' 50th ANNIVERSARY IN SHOW BUSINESS. The in-person autographs are treasures. This is the photo that Iron Eyes showed on the NICE PEOPLE TV Program. We salute you, Howard Moore, Ace Photographer 1981. On stage, left to right: Jock O'Mahoney, Lash LaRue, George Montgomery, Montie Montana. In stage: Eddie Dean, Rex Allen, Sr. Standing: Monte Hale, Tex Williams, Iron Eyes Cody, Dale Evans, Roy Rogers, Linda (Hayes) Crosby, Pat Buttram, Sunset Carson. Front row: The Sons of the Pioneers (Doc Denning, Roy Lanham, Dale Warren, Rusty Richards, and Luther Nallie).

GOLDEN BOOT AWARDS 1986 honored Tex Ritter, with Dorothy, Tom, and John on hand to accept the award. Above left, John Ritter displays the gold collar tips, pinned on by acting wardrobe mistress, Marietta Thompson. Roy Rogers, above, clowns around and sits on Bob Steele's knee, with Dale Evans and Victor French enjoying the antics. To the left, Iron Eyes with Gene Autry and Marietta.

spend.

Iron Eyes was honored with a Golden Boot in 1984. Several times I've been his guest at the "Boot Awards" and other activities; there is no way to measure the delight of being in the company of the ladies and gentlemen of filmdom.

William Campbell, Director of Fund Raising and Public Relations, heads the event. For information, write him at: Golden Boot Awards, 23300 Ventura Blvd., Woodland Hills, CA 91364.

Other occasions of longer duration are the film festivals scattered around the United States. Each lasts from one to four days and features movies pertaining to its particular genre, theme, or a combination of all.

For a daily fee of fifteen dollars or less, one can view the movies, meet some of the Stars who made those movies, take

pictures, get autographs, and buy memorabilia from hundreds of dealers who come from all over to buy, sell, and trade.

The Stars mill around with the rest of the fans, give panel discussions, sit in the theaters and watch their own movies with us.

Often there is a banquet for under twenty-five dollars per person on the last night when the Stars receive awards, and in turn may entertain with their beautifully diversified talents.

A word of advice: Watch for post festival depression! As in Knoxville, 1987, after a three-day high of being with the Stars, the adrenalin was still pumping. I met my childhood heroes and heroines and the time got shorter. The banquet of finality was held. A meal was shared; the nostalgic mood hovered. The evening drew to a close as Lew DeWitt (late of the Statler Brothers) stepped up to the microphone with guitar in hand and sang in that wonderfully high, quivery voice, a song about the day they tore down the Strand. I swallowed hard, choked back a tear, and gave a standing ovation to one who understood and shared what I felt.

The Stars began to leave; and then the friends who shared my interests also departed. A feeling swept over me - post festival depression.

My childhood has been relived. And now it's time to grow up again. More advice: Go home, develop the pictures, look at them and take a deep breath. Say a silent "thank you" to God for the people in those pictures. Get a good night's sleep and go back to work. Save my money and plan for the next time. It'll take a couple of weeks for the readjustment; but I will never be exactly as before. Now the film festival has become a part of me.

Wouldn't it be great if our children could have the western heroes like we had?

Addresses for information on the two festivals that I attend and enjoy more than words can express are: Memphis Film Festival, P.O. Box 40272, Memphis, TN 38174-0272; Riders of the Silver Screen Film Caravan, P.O. Box 3482, Knoxville, TN 37927.

CHAPTER 2

FILMOGRAPHY
and
MOVIE HISTORY IN PICTURES

1919
BACK TO GOD'S COUNTRY, Famous
   Players Lasky

1924
NORTH OF 36, Paramount
MINE WITH THE IRON DOOR, Principal

1925
THUNDERING HERD, Paramount
ELLA CINDERS, First National
HUMMING WIRES, MGM

1926
THE SCARLET LETTER, MGM
WAR PAINT, MGM
MAN TO THE WEST, MGM
BEN HUR, MGM

THE FLAMING FRONTIER, Universal

1927
BACK TO GOD'S COUNTRY, Universal
THE FRONTIERSMAN, MGM
WINNERS OF THE WILDERNESS, MGM
BUGLE CALL, MGM
ROSE MARIE, MGM
WITH SITTING BULL AT THE SPIRIT
   LAKE MASSACRE, Sunset

1928
WYOMING, MGM

1929
THE WOLF SONG, Paramount
SIOUX BLOOD, MGM

Iron Eyes with Harry Carey in ROSE MARIE, MGM, 1927.

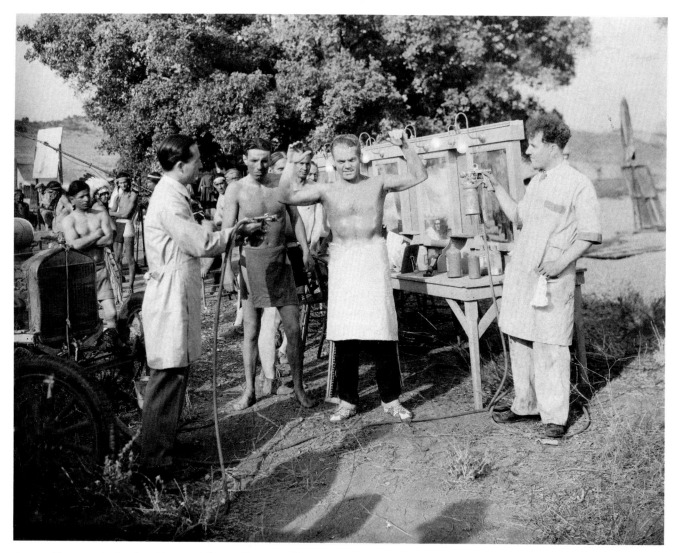

Iron Eyes next in line after Jimmy Cagney to be sprayed to look like an Indian in FINGER MAN, Warner–First National, 1930.

1930
THE BIG TRAIL, Fox
FINGER MAN, Warner-First National
THE INDIANS ARE COMING (serial), Universal
SANTA FE TRAIL, Warner-First National

1931
CIMARRON, RKO-Radio
FIGHTING CARAVANS aka BLAZING ARROWS, Paramount
OKLAHOMA JIM, Monogram
THE LIGHTNING WARRIOR (serial), Mascot

1932
WHISTLIN' DAN, Tiffany
THE RIDER OF DEATH VALLEY, Universal

THE GAY CABALLERO aka THE GAY BANDIT, Fox
THE RAINBOW TRAIL, Fox
TEXAS PIONEERS, Monogram
HEROES OF THE WEST (serial), Universal
CHANDU THE MAGICIAN, Fox
THE GOLDEN WEST, Fox

1933
KING OF THE ARENA, Universal
FIGHTING WITH KIT CARSON (serial), Mascot

1934
THE RETURN OF CHANDU (serial) Fox
MASSACRE, Griffin
THE RETURN OF CHANDU (feature from serial)

THE RETURN OF CHANDU, 1934 serial. Iron Eyes is on the right with Bela Lugosi in center.

Relaxing on a movie set. Left to right: Iron Eyes, Longplume Cody (Iron Eyes' father), Silvermoon Cody (Iron Eyes' brother). George O'Brien is facing them. Noble Johnson is on the right.

CHANDU ON THE MAGIC ISLE (feature from serial)
THE SCARLET LETTER, Majestic
WAGON WHEELS, Paramount
THE THUNDERING HERD, Paramount
YOUNG EAGLES (serial), First Division
THE MAN FROM UTAH, Monogram

1935
TOLL OF THE DESERT, Commodore
THE MIRACLE RIDER (serial), Mascot
ROSE MARIE, MGM
THE FARMER TAKES A WIFE, Fox

1936
TREACHERY RIDES THE RANGE, Warner Brothers
THE PHANTOM RIDER (serial), Universal
RIDE RANGER RIDE, Republic
CUSTER'S LAST STAND (serial), Stage & Screen
OVERLAND TELEGRAPH, MGM
CHARGE OF THE LIGHT BRIGADE, Warner Brothers
RHYTHM ON THE RANGE, Paramount

1937
RIDERS OF THE WHISTLING SKULL, Republic
OLD LOUISIANA aka LOUISIANA GAL, Crescent
WILD WEST DAYS (serial), Universal

THE PLAINSMAN, Paramount
PRAIRIE THUNDER, Warner Brothers

1938
FLAMING FRONTIERS (serial), Universal
THE LONE RANGER (serial), Republic
STAMPEDE, Paramount
HAWK OF THE WILDERNESS (serial),
    Republic
LOST ISLAND OF KIOGA (TV-feature
    from HAWK OF THE WILDERNESS
    serial)

1939
CRASHING THRU, Grand National
STAGECOACH, United Artists
UNION PACIFIC, Paramount
THE OREGON TRAIL (serial), Universal
OVERLAND WITH KIT CARSON (serial),
    Columbia
COLORADO, Republic

YOUNG BILL HICKOK, Republic
UNTAMED, Paramount
ZORRO'S FIGHTING LEGION (serial),
    Republic
SUSANNAH OF THE MOUNTIES, 20th
    Century Fox

1940
GREEN HELL, Universal
MY LITTLE CHICKADEE, Universal
YOUNG BUFFALO BILL, Republic
OVERLAND MAIL, Monogram
BOOMTOWN, MGM
NORTHWEST MOUNTED POLICE,
    Paramount
PONY POST, Universal
NORTHWEST PASSAGE, MGM
WINNERS OF THE WEST (serial),
    Universal

RHYTHM ON THE RANGE, Paramount, 1936. Silvermoon Cody, Iron Eyes' brother, is holding peace pipe and talking with Crooner-Actor Bing Crosby. Iron Eyes is standing in right background.

36

TREACHERY RIDES THE RANGE, Warner Brothers, 1936. Monte Blue is wearing hat, with All-American Jim Thorpe to his right. At the top, the arrow to the left points to Iron Eyes' brother, Silvermoon, while the arrow to the right points to his brother, Red Star. Iron Eyes stands fifth from right.

FLAMING FRONTIERS, Universal serial, 1938. Western actor and former football star, Johnny Mack Brown, is being detained by Iron Eyes.

YOUNG BUFFALO BILL, Republic, 1940. Iron Eyes is shown with Roy Rogers.

WINNERS OF THE WEST, Universal serial, 1940. Chief Yowlachie is shown in center with Harry Woods to his right and Charlie Stevens to his left. Iron Eyes is standing on the end next to Stevens.

1941
THE SEA WOLF, Warner Brothers
SADDLEMATES, Republic
OUTLAWS OF THE CHEROKEE TRAIL,
    Republic
KING OF THE TEXAS RANGERS (serial),
    Republic
THEY DIED WITH THEIR BOOTS ON,
    Warner Brothers
WESTERN UNION, 20th Century Fox
IN OLD CHEYENNE, Republic
THE ROUND UP, Paramount

1942
RIDE'EM COWBOY, Universal
PERILS OF THE ROYAL MOUNTED
    (serial), Columbia
KING OF THE STALLIONS, Monogram
SPRINGTIME IN THE ROCKIES,
    20th Century Fox

DAWN ON THE GREAT DIVIDE,
    Monogram
OVERLAND MAIL (serial), Universal
THE VALLEY OF THE SUN, RKO-Radio
MY GAL SAL, 20th Century Fox

1943
THE OUTLAW, United Artists

1944
BLACK ARROW (serial), Columbia

1945
THEY WERE EXPENDABLE, MGM

1946
UNDER NEVADA SKIES, Republic
THE PLAINSMAN AND THE LADY,
    Republic
MY DARLING CLEMENTINE, 20th Century
    Fox

RIDE'EM COWBOY, Universal, 1941. Iron Eyes is in the center with Bud Abbott on the left and Lou Costello on the right.

UNCONQUERED, Paramount, 1947. Iron Eyes is on the left with C. B. DeMille and Jay Silverheels who is best known for his portrayal as Tonto in The Lone Ranger movies and TV series.

1947
THE LAST ROUNDUP, Columbia
BOWERY BUCKAROOS, Monogram
THE SENATOR WAS INDISCREET,
    Universal
UNCONQUERED, Paramount

1948
THE GALLANT LEGION, Republic
INDIAN AGENT, RKO-Radio
THE PALEFACE, Paramount
FORT APACHE, RKO-Radio
TRAIN TO ALCATRAZ, Republic
THE DUDE GOES WEST, Allied Artists
BLOOD ON THE MOON, RKO-Radio

1949
THE COWBOY AND THE INDIANS,
    Columbia
MASSACRE RIVER, Allied Artists

SAND, 20th Century Fox
SHE WORE A YELLOW RIBBON, Argosy-
    RKO
MRS. MIKE, United Artists
TULSA, Eagle Lion/Pathe
DAUGHTER OF THE WEST, Film Classics

1950
COMANCHE TERRITORY, Universal-
    International
BROKEN ARROW, 20th Century Fox
CHEROKEE UPRISING, Monogram
NORTH OF THE GREAT DIVIDE, Republic
CALIFORNIA PASSAGE, Republic
THE IROQUOIS TRAIL, United Artists
WAGONMASTER, Argosy-RKO
THE DEVIL'S DOORWAY, MGM
I KILLED GERONIMO, Eagle-Lion
ANNIE GET YOUR GUN, MGM

Iron Eyes in INDIAN AGENT, 1948, an RKO Tim Holt picture.

MRS. MIKE, United Artists, 1949. Shown from left to right: Evelyn Keyes, Dick Powell, Chief Yowlachie, Iron Eyes Cody and Victor Daniels (Thunder Cloud).

NORTH OF THE GREAT DIVIDE, Republic, 1950, Iron Eyes with Roy Rogers.

42

1951
FORT DEFIANCE, United Artists
TOMAHAWK, Universal-International
LAST OUTPOST, Paramount

1952
SOUND OFF, Columbia
MEET ME AT THE FAIR, Universal
NIGHT RAIDERS, Monogram
FORT OSAGE, Monogram
RED MOUNTAIN, Paramount
APACHE COUNTRY, Columbia
THE BIG SKY, RKO-Radio
LOST IN ALASKA, Universal
SON OF PALEFACE, Paramount
MONTANA BELLE, RKO-Radio

1953
THE SAVAGE aka WAR BONNET,
    Paramount
FAST COMPANY, MGM
ARROWHEAD, Paramount

THE LAST OUTPOST, Paramount, 1951, with Ronald Reagan.

LOST IN ALASKA, Universal, 1952. Left to right: Bud Abbott, Tom Ewell, Iron Eyes Cody, Mitzi Green, and Lou Costello.

FAST COMPANY, MGM, 1953. Polly Bergen, Howard Keel, and Iron Eyes Cody.

CHARGE AT FEATHER RIVER (3-D), Warner Brothers

1954
ARROW IN THE DUST, Allied Artists
YELLOW TOMAHAWK, United Artists
SITTING BULL, United Artists

1955
WHITE FEATHER, 20th Century Fox
APACHE AMBUSH, Columbia
DAVY CROCKETT, KING OF THE WILD FRONTIER, Disney

1956
THE WILD DAKOTAS, Associated Films
WESTWARD HO THE WAGONS, Disney
THE LAST WAGON, 20th Century Fox
COMANCHE, United Artists
THE SEARCHERS, Warner Brothers

1957
GUN FOR A COWARD, Universal
RUN OF THE ARROW, RKO
RIDE OUT FOR REVENGE, United Artists

SITTING BULL, United Artists, 1954. Crazy Horse (Iron Eyes Cody) and Sitting Bull (Carrol Naish).

44

APACHE AMBUSH, Columbia, 1955.

WESTWARD HO THE WAGONS, Disney, 1956, Iron Eyes with Fess Parker, left.

LIGHT IN THE FOREST, Disney, 1958, with Fess Parker, left.

1958
GUN FEVER, United Artists
LIGHT IN THE FOREST, Disney
TONKA, Disney

1959
ALIAS JESSE JAMES, United Artists
THE OREGON TRAIL, 20th Century Fox

1960
HELLER IN PINK TIGHTS, Paramount

1963
BLACK GOLD, Warner Brothers

SAVAGE SAM, Disney

1965
THE GREAT SIOUX MASSACRE, Columbia

1966
NEVADA SMITH, Paramount

1967
THE FASTEST GUITAR ALIVE, MGM
HONDO AND THE APACHE, MGM

1968
SOMETHING FOR A LONELY MAN,
    Universal/NBC-TV

BLACK GOLD, Warner Brothers, 1963. Iron Eyes Cody and Diane McBain.

1970
A MAN CALLED HORSE, National General
THE COCKEYED COWBOYS OF CALICO
   COUNTY, Universal
EL CONDOR, National General

1975
HEARTS OF THE WEST, MGM-United
   Artists

1976
RETURN OF A MAN CALLED HORSE,
   United Artists
THE QUEST, Columbia/NBC-TV

1977
GRAYEAGLE, American International

EL CONDOR, National General, 1970, with
Lee Van Cleef.

THE COCKEYED COWBOYS OF CALICO COUNTY, 1970. Cast picture. Iron Eyes was the only Indian. Shown back row, left to right: Wally Cox, Henry Jones, Donald Barry, Noah Beery, Jr., Stubby Kaye, Hamilton Camp, Jack Elam and Mickey Rooney. Front row, left to right: Jack Cassidy, Dan Blocker, Nanette Fabray, Jim Backus and Iron Eyes Cody, sitting on floor.

GRAYEAGLE, American-International, 1977, with Ben Johnson.

THE QUEST, NBC TV, Columbia, 1976, with Will (Sugarfoot) Hutchins.

MEANWHILE, BACK AT THE RANCH, Rancho Films

1979
THEY WORE TEN GALLON HATS, Western Series

1986
ERNEST GOES TO CAMP, Disney

CHAPTER 3
ON THE TRAIL OF IRON EYES

Iron Eyes is shown here receiving an award from Los Angeles Mayor, Tom Bradley.

The life pattern of our hero, Iron Eyes Cody, could be termed, "a busy man gets the job done." Known throughout the world as a symbol of the American Spirit, he surely must be nearing ten feet tall to reach his heights of attainment.

To know all the organizations, meetings, and ceremonies he attends, one would have to follow him around the clock with a notebook, constantly mapping the way. To keep up with this man is a job in itself. A few times I have tried to match steps with him over a three or four day period, and let me say that it's not easy.

A tireless worker, Iron Eyes supports numerous causes (especially those for children, handicapped, and underprivileged) with his time as well as his money. He devotes himself to a wide variety of civic and community clubs. Highly respected, he serves as a trustee on boards, and he chairs and holds together many groups.

Iron Eyes believes that to achieve is nothing if the achievement is not used to help others. And he surely does help others, wherever the most good can be done.

In 1935, Iron Eyes helped found the Los Angeles Indian Center. The Center is concerned with all phases of Indian community life, the social, cultural, and economic well-being of the Indian people -- health, jobs, census, political laws, mental attitudes, education, welfare, and human rights. It publishes a monthly newspaper (for Indians) called "Talking Leaf" that discusses all the issues. Iron Eyes writes a regular column in it called "Little Big Horn News." Now a lifetime member, Iron Eyes continues to stress its importance to the area.

Iron Eyes was one of four founders of The Little Big Horn Club, known since 1963 as The Little Big Horn Association. This is a social service Indian community club that promotes cultural programs and holds fund raisers for various causes throughout the United States. As President for 12 years, Iron Eyes takes the lead in settling disputes with his authority and wisdom.

National American Indian Day is a powwow of fellowship and celebration with events for young and old. It was founded in 1914 by Dr. Arthur C. Parker (father-in-law to Iron Eyes), in Congressional Proclamation. 1987 marked the 27th year year that Iron Eyes had guided the Los Angeles Indian Center and The Little Big Horn Club in hosting National American Indian Day in Los Angeles on the second Sunday in September. Thousands attend this event each year. It was Birdie, his wife, who instituted the National Indian Day observance in California in 1934, with Sycamore Grove Park/Highland Park as the initial meeting place.

For fourteen years Iron Eyes served on the Los Angeles City Indian Board; and he is in his twelfth year on the Los Angeles City/County Native American Indian Commission. The purpose of this group is to accurately count the Indians so that the proper amount of federal funding will reach the Los Angeles area. Iron Eyes and Lincoln Billedeaux were the first two commissioners sworn in when the duel-commission was formed in 1976.

Iron Eyes represented the Los Angeles Supervisors when he presented the Los Angeles City Resolution to the Thorpe

Dedicating the Jim Thorpe Park, Hawthorne, CA.

family during the dedication of the Jim Thorpe Park in Hawthorne, California on February 23, 1974. (Jim Thorpe was in the 1912 Olympics. He won gold medals in both the decathlon and pentathlon. The medals were taken away when officials charged him with being a professional baseball player.) Iron Eyes then donated a 1914 Jim Thorpe football (that Jim had given to Iron Eyes' Moosehead Museum in 1940.) The football is now enclosed in a glass case with some of Jim Thorpe's medals.

Each year near Thanksgiving, Iron Eyes joins Litton Flying Club in a pilgrimage of thirty light airplanes to deliver turkeys, tons of other foods, and warm clothing to needy Indian reservations.

Using an eagle feather, Iron Eyes blesses the gifts and the airplanes. As a liaison with the Indian world, he says, "The Indians gave the white man the first Thanksgiving. Now it is good that the white man remembers and reciprocates."

Litton Industries contributes prizes as fund raisers; foods are bought with the funds collected. Over a hundred club members solicit the needed items. Flight and fuel expenses, and any rental fees fo the planes are paid by the pilots and co-pilots. Club dues pay for publicity. The club was incorporated in 1970 and has become a recognized supplier of human needs, choosing a different tribe to assist each year.

In one way or another, Iron Eyes has helped every Indian reservation in the United States and more individual people than one can imagine.

While visiting the United States in 1979, the Emperor and Empress of Japan requested to meet three people: Iron Eyes Cody, John Wayne, and Charlton Heston. Los Angeles Mayor, Tom Bradley arranged a luncheon for the group. It was the last time John Wayne was out of the hospital before his death.

With pride in the memory of his dear friend, John Wayne, Iron Eyes was present on July 22, 1984, for the unveiling and dedication of the John Wayne Statue, entitled "The Horseman." It is a 21-foot, 5-ton bronze sculpture by a great artist, Harry Jackson, and is located at the Great Western Savings Plaza, in Los Angeles.

Iron Eyes with John Wayne at dinner for Emperor of Japan.

The Postmaster General sent a special invitation to Iron Eyes for the ceremony dedicating the Frederic Remington Stamp and the unveiling of the "Coming Through the Rye" statue on October 9, 1981, at the National Cowboy Hall of Fame in Oklahoma City. In turn, Iron Eyes donated, to that fine establishment, some of his Andy Anders' Carvings and an Eagle Feather Headdress in honor of his father, Thomas Longplume Cody.

The years have certainly been full for Iron Eyes; many things are coming together for the good.

On Friday, April 6, 1984, at Red Clay State Historic Park in Cleveland, Tennessee, the Chiefs of the Eastern and Western Bands of the Cherokee Nation met together for the first time since they were separated 147 years previously. At that time, federal armies forced most of them to Oklahoma in the winter. Many died on that journey. Some of the Indians escaped to North Carolina and formed a separate

Black Belt – Karate
Boy Scouts Life Member of the Verdugo Council
Boy Scouts 40 Year Award
Buffalo Bill Award
Distinction Award from the Hays/ Lodge Pole School
Documentary Awards for "The American Indian Before the White Man" and "The American Indian After the White Man"
End of Trail Award 1986
Ethnic Fellowship Award
Friends of Hart Park Award
Gift of Sight Award
Golden Mask Award for Acting Ability
Golden Boot Award 1984
Golden Star Halo Award

Gold Star Award for 50 Years in Show Business 1982 (It should have been 60 years)
Honorary Mayor of Burbank
Honorary Member Stuntmen's Hall of Fame
Honor by FACT (Facility for Animal Care and Treatment) 1987
Indian of the Year 1984
Iron Eyes Cody Testimonial Dinner by the L.A. City/County Native American Indian Commission
Key to City of New York
Man of the West 1982 (from the American Indian & Cowboy Artists Society of San Dimas, CA., for people who have a willingness to demonstrate that two cultures can work together in harmony.)

Iron Eyes and Bob Hope received awards in 1978 from Donald Douglas, Jr. (of McDonald-Douglas Aircraft), Council President of Great Western Council, Boy Scouts of America.

National Chairman of the Narcotics Prevention Task Force 1975

Navajo Code Talkers Commendation 1986 (The Japanese military never solved the riddle of the messages in Navajo. The Code Talkers just talked Navajo backwards.)

Press Conference with Iron Eyes 1985 (Nashville, TN)

Resolution Scroll from the City of Los Angeles for his work on behalf of Indian traditions (signed by all 15 Councilmen, including 1964 Olympic Gold Medalist Billy Mills)

Sagamore of the Wabash from the State of Indiana

Unknown Indian Award

Western Walk of Fame 1985

Who's Who in the World 1987/1988 (The Marquis)

Iron Eyes Cody Day, March 26, 1987 (Bakersfield, CA)

There is no end to his work, so the awards will continue to find him.

Iron Eyes serves on the Advisory Committee for The American Indian Registry For The Performing Arts. When its Chairman Emeritus, Will Sampson, Creek Indian actor, passed away June 3, 1987, the Registry gave a special benefit dance for him. Iron Eyes was Honorary Chairman for this event. The purpose of this non-profit organization is to help young Indian actors and performers. Address for information: 3330 Barham Blvd., Suite 208, Los Angeles, CA 90068.

At times, one may have difficulty getting in touch with Iron Eyes Cody; this man is on the go. He could be attending any number of meetings, possibly one of these:

Audio-Visual Broadcasting Systems (Director)

American Federation of Television and Radio Artists (Director)

American Indian Film Festival

American Indian Free Clinic (Honorary Member)

American Foundation of Art

American Indian Week

Boy Scouts of America

Confederated Tribes of American Indians

City/County Indian Commission

California League of Senior Citizens

Chuck Wagon Trailers

Energy Fair

Ecology Club of America

Film Welfare League

Grand Council American Indian

Hope Ranch (Fort Peck Reservation)

International Academy of Psychic Artists

Little Big Horn Association (Founder and President)

Los Angeles Indian Center (Founder and Life Member)

Los Angeles County Library Association (Director and Photographer)

Los Angeles Karate Association (Black Belt)

Maskers Club

Motion Picture Council

Southwest Museum (Trustee)

Saints and Sinners

Screen Actors Guild (Director)

Westerners (Director, Photographer, Chief of Smoke Signals)

WeTip (We Turn In Pushers)

Y.M.C.A.

Often Iron Eyes is too busy to eat. As he puts it, "I've always been a busy person! Even as a child, I was often just too busy to eat."

The Roosevelt Hotel was packed on October 11, 1986, when friends from all over came to formally install Iron Eyes to a four-year term as Chairman of the Hollywood Appreciation Society which meets twice a year. Iron Eyes captivated the audience each time he returned to the microphone. The motive of the Hollywood Appreciation Society is to uplift the name of Hollywood in the eyes of the public. The Association honors anyone in the film world who believes that Hollywood is not dead. They promote clean wholesome movies such as Hollywood used to produce.

The author was honored to be invited to the festivities, seated between Jock O'Mahoney (TV's Range Rider) and John E. Church of Aerospace Corporation; and doubly honored when Iron Eyes announced this book and introduced me as his co-author.

He asked me to say a few words which I was unprepared for; but I made some comments and concluded with, "We all love Iron Eyes, don't we?" The applause nearly brought down the roof!

In addition to visiting 45 to 50 cities each year for Keep America Beautiful; attending meetings or organizations, clubs and powwows; participating in 40 or more parades as Grand Marshal, Division Mar-

shal, Celebrity Guest; and promoting fund raisers; this popular Master of Ceremonies lectures against alcoholism; works for all Native American causes; makes special tapes for the blind; and still finds time to make one movie per year--if he finds one to his liking.

Iron Eyes' latest movie, ERNEST GOES TO CAMP (Disney), also stars Jim (Vern, knowhutimean?) Varney and Victoria Racimo. This is a clean, family-type show, filmed for the most part in Montgomery Bell Park near Nashville, Tennessee. Theater release date was April, 1987, and the net income first run was 23 million dollars, a definite plus.

The two extravaganza parades to which most of us look forward with growing excitement are the Rose Parade and the Hollywood Christmas Parade. (Numerous Stars of all ages promote various projects and send good wishes to all their fans.)

Iron Eyes has ridden in the Hollywood

Screen Actors Guild, Board of Directors Meeting, 1978. Iron Eyes on front row, right end. Photo by Douglas Hill.

Christmas Parade for 30 years consecutively, and intermittently, since it was made official in 1924, as the Santa Claus Lane Parade.

The 1986 spotlight of the parade represented Resistol Hats' salute to and support of Gene Autry's Western Heritage Museum. Resistol makes the handsome white hats seen on so many of the western heroes.

In 1987, Iron Eyes was honored in

Ready for the 1986 Hollywood Christmas Parade. From left: Iron Eyes, Eddie Dean, Monte Hale, Pat Buttram, Richard Farnsworth and Clayton Moore.

Rose Parade 1976. Iron Eyes is riding Montie Montana's horse, George. Photo by Bob Plunkett.

Rose Parade 1975. Iron Eyes is wearing double trailer war bonnet on float of flowers shaped as a double trailer.

Pawnee Bill, Tom Mix, and Iron Eyes, ready for the Santa Claus Lane Parade, circa 1936. Photo courtesy of M. G. Norris and David L. Morgan.

58

Pasadena for 37 years with the Rose Parade; 36 on horseback and one on a float.

Iron Eyes says he really enjoys judging beauty contests. One he judged recently was the Jerry Lewis Muscular Dystrophy Beauty Contest on August 24, 1986. "A quitter never wins, and a winner never quits" was the appropriate slogan for this event.

As a member of the Uwipi Medicine Man's Society, Iron Eyes officiates at weddings. He can bless the union but cannot issue the diploma which must be signed by an official such as a Justice of the Peace.

A very special Indian wedding that he was invited to was the huge, traditional Ojibwa Ceremony of Mel and Lynda Pervais in June, 1985. A portion of this ceremony was later shown on a PHIL DONAHUE SHOW about various types of traditional weddings. Iron Eyes' voice could be heard singing with the Head Drum.

5858 SUNSET BOULEVARD • P.O. BOX 710 • LOS ANGELES, CALIFORNIA 90078

July 7, 1987

Dear Ms. Thompson:

I have known Iron Eyes Cody for many years and he has worked in a good number of my films. He is a fine actor and humanitarian and I am proud to call him my friend.

Iron Eyes has also generously contributed to the Gene Autry Western Heritage Museum and we are most appreciative of his support in this area.

He is truly an outstanding American and credit to our great nation.

Warmest personal regards,

Gene Autry

Ms. Marietta Thompson
Route 1, Box 114
Tuckerman, Arkansas 72473

Iron Eyes, assisted by Sandy Redhawk, officiated at the Indian wedding of Robin Abrams Duarte, 1982.

Excitement is growing as the Gene Autry Western Heritage Museum becomes reality. Groundbreaking was November 12, 1986, at Griffith Park. Stars and fans are anxious to share the mood of the Old West, including the movie era. Donations to the museum from Iron Eyes include a $10,000 lifesize bronze bust of himself, sculpted by artist, Ken Ball; a peace pipe, beaded bag, and several paintings.

Iron Eyes practically lives on planes and loves flying. In January, 1987, he flew by private plane to Oklahoma to present an Iron Eyes Cody Peace Medal to Hollis Roberts, Chief of the Choctaw Nation. The Indian was in turn honored himself by being made an Honorary Choctaw Chief, along with Lee Cannon who received the same honor. Mr. Cannon is Press Secretary of the Navajo Nations and has worked with Indian tribes across the United States. Those of us who have been calling Iron Eyes "Chief" have now been vindicated. An Indian holds the Chief in such high esteem that he cannot allow himself to be called by the name unless he is so entitled.

On May 9, 1987, it was off to London, England for the dedication of a

Life size bronze bust of Iron Eyes by Ken Ball.

bronze plaque honoring Buffalo Bill. On hand to do the unveiling was William Garlow Cody, grandson of Buffalo Bill. Iron Eyes wore the same beaded buckskins that his father, Longplume, wore when Buffalo Bill's Wild West was in London in 1904.

As the first stop on a seven-year tour, the 1887 opening of the Wild West Exhibition at Earls Court took "untamed"

There must be a good show going on!

The look of the eighties: A new white tuxedo for formal occasions.

America to England in a way never before presented. England has never forgotten Buffalo Bill and his troup of Indians.

ANNOUNCING: Iron Eyes has a new toy! In search of him? Look for the person hidden behind the video camera. That will be Iron Eyes. First it was an RCA, then a Quasar, and now it's a Sony. Those "toy" companies sure do spark the interest!

CHAPTER 4

QUALITY IN THE NAME

When the name of Iron Eyes Cody is attached to an object or an event, people take notice. For instance, his reputation of "good sport" preceded him, when on June 10, 1982, The International Guiding Eyes and the Los Angeles Indian Centers, Inc. combined forces to present a Celebrity Roast Dinner in tribute to Iron Eyes Cody, the most famous face in America.

Los Angeles American Indian Center
and
International Guiding Eyes
Presents
A Celebrity Roast
for
"Iron Eyes Cody"
Thursday, June 10, 1982 - 6:30 p.m.
Sportsmans Lodge
12833 Ventura Boulevard
Studio City, California 91604
Donation $35.

The successful fund raiser at thirty-five dollars per person was held at the Sportsmans Lodge in Studio City, CA, to a packed house of movie stars, Indian dancers, western recording artists, and politicians. Eddie Dean, Joanne and Monte Hale, Harvey Parry, Tim O'Sullivan, Ken Hahn, Duke Lee, Johnny Grant, Tenaya Torres (Mazola Corn Oil girl) were among the handsome and beautiful in attendance.

Before a person's likeness can be placed on a postage stamp, the U. S. Postal Service requires that the person be deceased. But Keep America Beautiful chose to honor a living person with the issue of the First Edition National Environmental Stamp which was introduced on August 16, 1982. Millions of his fans applauded that Iron Eyes Cody was chosen. Envelopes were issued for those who collect First Day Covers.

Napkins at Iron Eyes' roast depicted the "Wooden Indian."

A nice addition for stamp collectors was the October 7, 1982 issuing of the 20-cent U. S. Postage Stamp, "St. Francis of Assisi," which could be added to or correlated with the Iron Eyes Cody envelope and stamp. St. Francis of Assisi and Iron Eyes both cried for the environment. Any Indian postage stamp also related well with the envelope.

62

— OFFICIAL FIRST DAY COVER —
Keep America Beautiful Foundation

The handsome painting is the work of Bob Timberlake of Lexington, North Carolina, an artist nationally acclaimed for realism, simple beauty and vision. His career is emphasized in the KAB official announcement, along with a picture of the stamp and a photo of the artist with Iron Eyes.

Address for the $5.00 Iron Eyes Cody Stamp: Keep America Beautiful, National Environmental Stamp, 516 North Wrenn Street, High Point, N.C. 27262.

Bob Timberlake creating the Iron Eyes Cody Stamp. Photo by Les.

On April 20, 1983, Iron Eyes received the 1,761st star on the Hollywood Walk of Fame. Los Angeles Chamber of Commerce representatives, Johnny Grant, Bill Welsh and William F. Hertz made the dedication and presentation to a most deserving recipient, sponsored by The Noteworthy Paper Company and Keep America Beautiful, Inc.

Artist John Steele is commended for his suggestion of the location: near the corner of Hollywood Boulevard and Chero-

THE WHITE HOUSE

WASHINGTON

May 5, 1983

Dear Iron Eyes:

It is a pleasure to congratulate you on your induction into the Hollywood Walk of Fame.

This tribute reflects your unique contribution to the Motion Picture Industry. You've done so much to preserve the American Indian Heritage and culture through your work in films. Your superb portrayal in the famous "Keep America Beautiful" commercials has made millions of Americans stop and think about the danger of losing our natural beauty. Your efforts have helped turn the tide, and America is looking greener and cleaner once more.

You truly are a great American, and I'm proud to know you.

With best wishes and, again, congratulations.

Sincerely,

Ronald Reagan

Mr. Iron Eyes Cody
Keep America Beautiful, Inc.
Hollywood Roosevelt Hotel
7000 Hollywood Boulevard
Hollywood, California 90028

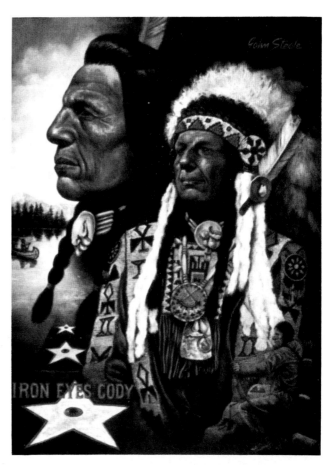

Painting by John Steele, commemorating Iron Eyes' induction to the Hollywood Walk of Fame.

kee Avenue, a fitting place for a Cree-Cherokee Man.

The 2½ mile stretch of sidewalk contains brass-rimmed, pink colored terrazzo, star-shaped plaques, honoring heroes of the theater, movies, radio, TV and music. Of 500 nominated each year, only 3 to 4 per cent are selected. Installation cost of a star is currently $3,500.

For years Iron Eyes had said "no" to having his star placed because of the unclean, unkept appearance of the walk. But through the achievement of Los Angeles Councilwoman, Peggy Stevenson, Hollywood Boulevard was cleaned up with restored dignity.

On this particular day, a torrent rain fell on Los Angeles just as Iron Eyes' star was being unveiled. It was as if the rain was sent to finalize the clean-up operation.

IRON EYES CODY'S INDUCTION
INTO THE HOLLYWOOD WALK OF
FAME AS SEEN BY THE PEN OF
ARTIST, JOHN STEELE.

Everyone got wet, but no one left. That in itself was a tribute to Iron Eyes. However, Pat Buttram got sick from the dampness and had to be hospitalized. During his fever, the Great Spirit gave Pat a vision of Gene Autry painting his old, worn out boots with gold paint and giving them as awards; the result of which became the Golden Boot Awards that very year with Pat as the first Master of Ceremonies. Anyone who has the opportunity to hear the wit of Pat Buttram is fortunate indeed.

Iron Eyes is partially responsible for the Boot Awards because never before in history had it rained on anyone being inducted into the Hollywood Walk of Fame.

He was the fourth Indian so inducted; the other three were Nipo T. Strongheart, Monte Blue and Jay Silverheels.

The Montebello Country Club, Montebello, CA, was the setting for the Iron Eyes Cody First Annual Celebrity Golf Classic on Thursday, May 31, 1984.

The tournament for the New Center for Development of Potential of the Handicapped was hosted by Bob Beltran, along with Shirley and Paul Zaharia, founders of CENDEVOPH Handicapped Foundation. Entry fee was $150 each for a limited 144 players; non-golfers paid $100 each, which included entertainment and an awards dinner. Entertainment was provided by Lalo Guerrero, A Touch of Latin, and the Bonner Family.

Special guest stars were: Vic Tabac (from ALICE), Fred Williamson (The Hammer), Jim Brown, Bill Russell, Lawrence McCutcheon (NFL pro), James Harris (NFL pro), James Shorter (NFL pro), Harrold Carrold (NFL pro), Enos Cabel (baseball pro), Sidney Williams (NFL pro), Alton Duhon (U.S. senior golf champ), and Bob Beltran (state of California champ).

IRON EYES CODY CELEBRITY GOLF CLASSIC TOURNAMENT IS FOR THE NEW CENTER FOR DEVELOPMENT OF POTENTIAL OF THE HANDICAPPED.

Iron Eyes showing his Medal.. Fred's Photography.

Often times when an Indian Chief was friendly with the white man, the Indian was given a presidential peace medal as a reward. Each medal had the president's likeness on one side and a message of significance on the reverse. For instance, Abraham Lincoln's issue showed agriculture as an alternative to scalping.

Keep America Beautiful, Inc. decided if a president could give an Indian a medal, so could an Indian give a medal to the President of the United States, or to anyone whose service should be recognized.

The three-inch medallion was designed by artist, John Steele; and in 1984, the first issue of Iron Eyes Cody Peace Medals were struck. Sioux Medicine Man, Frank Foolscrow, blessed them.

Marietta Thompson with Iron Eyes. "The ties on my peace medal are cut from a hide that was blessed many years ago by Sioux Medicine Man, Bill 'Eagle Feather' Sweigman. Each time I wear it something good always happens to me." ...Marietta

Ben Johnson receiving Iron Eyes Cody Peace Medal, in recognition of selection as 1987 Indian of the Year. Photo by Cindy R. Peery.

Recipients of the Iron Eyes Cody Peace Medal awarded to those who have involved themselves in BROTHERHOOD, UNITY and FRIENDSHIP are: Will Geer, Roger Powers, Billy Mills, Keenan Wynn, Charles Schriener III, Ross Swimmer, Robert Youngdeer, Ted Shinning Warrior, Peter McDonald, Joel Carlson, John Philip Clark, Jr., John Hinchcliffe, Rod McHague, John E. Echohawk, John Kniefchief, President Ronald Reagan, Connie Stevens, Pope John Paul II, Tom Bradley, Peterson Zah, Melvin Malone, Marietta Thompson, Wilma Mankiller, Mel Pervais, Mr. Pervais (father of Mel), Ann Louise Willie, Ted Murphy, John Glenn, Lee Cannon, W. Clement Stone, Ken Childs, A. David Lester, Bob Ferguson, Phillip Martin, Frank Steve, Ken Ball, Sammy "Tonekei" White, Ben Williams, Hollis Roberts, Tom Constantino, Reno Johnson, Ben Johnson, Ned McWherter, Richard Fulton and A. C. Lyles.

CHAPTER 5

A BETTER WORLD
BECAUSE OF ONE INDIAN

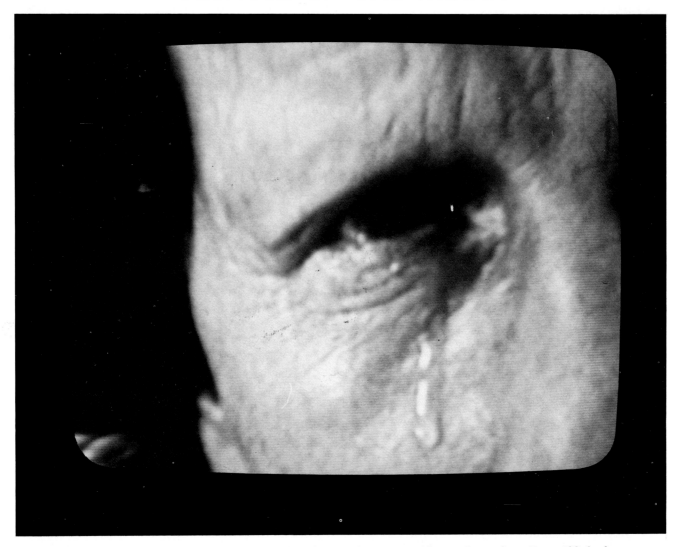

Photo from Iron Eyes' private collection. Courtesy Keep America Beautiful, Inc.

With the shedding of a single tear, Iron Eyes reached America with the message of Keep America Beautiful; via television that tear spread worldwide to an estimated 24 billion home impressions. Quite a record!

When first approached by Keep America Beautiful over twenty years ago, Iron Eyes refused to do the crying Indian because Indian men don't cry. They have sadness in their hearts, but express those feelings in sad and wailing songs. Also, a canoe was too small to paddle in San Francisco Bay. It would probably sink; and if it did sink, the buckskin outfit would hold water and cause him to drown.

Finally in 1968, after two years of repeated requests from Lady Bird Johnson, and an offer to do two versions--one with a tear and one without, Iron Eyes decided to do it. He agreed to wear a "Mae West," a type of inflatable vest; but he didn't try it out. And would you believe that after the filming, he tried the thing and it didn't even work!

But cry from one eye? He had to

think on that. On a hospital visit with some sick children, he noticed a fifteen year old girl crying; and her tears came from one eye. When questioned about it, she said that was the only way she had ever cried. So he thought it might be possible; maybe he could do it.

Iron Eyes tried thinking emotional thoughts, and he even looked directly into the sun. That brought tears, but from both eyes. Various suggestions were made to him about what to put in his eyes to cause tears, but Iron Eyes refused them because he was nearly blinded from glycerine in a sloppy makeup job during the filming of A MAN CALLED HORSE. Iron Eyes' choice was Visine. Next time he'll use syrup. The script called for him to paddle in the canoe, then to stand and have garbage thrown at his feet. The impact and strength of that tear resulted in the unbelievable instant success of a commercial, which won three Clio Awards, the Oscar of advertising.

Keep America Beautiful is a national nonpartisan, non-profit, public service organization which was founded in 1953. It is dedicated to the reduction of litter through the improvement of waste handling practices, and beautification by volunteers of professional quality in conservation and recycling.

The principal program, The Clean Community System works to change negative attitudes. Over 350 cities in 40 states and 7 other countries now participate. England's Queen Elizabeth and the Queen Mother) honored KAB in 1981 with a special award at "The Queen Mother's 80th Birthday Awards" at St. James Palace in London. She serves as patron of KAB's affiliate, the Keep Britain Tidy Group.

In connection with Keep America Beautiful, a pilot program was begun in

Photo from Iron Eyes' private collection. Courtesy Keep America Beautiful, Inc.

1984 in the United States as Public Lands Day. U.S. Senator, Dale Bumpers of Arkansas introduced a bill that was passed to establish a National Lands Cleanup Day on Saturday after Labor Day each year. Ninety-five per cent of the country cleans up on that day; but each state was given the option of an earlier date due to weather conditions that prevail in certain locations during that particular time period.

Greer's Ferry Lake and Little Red River Cleanup in Arkansas serve as a first-place, award-winning national model for the program. Thousands of volunteers cover 276 miles of shoreline and 40 miles of highways in the clean-up project. After all the work is done, everyone is invited to a massive fish fry and entertainment extravaganza at the Narrows Park, with food and entertainment furnished by area merchants and entertainers.

Honorable guests of the National Lands Cleanup Day in 1986 included Senator Bumpers, Ramona and Grandpa Jones (from the TV show Hee Haw and the world famous Grand Ole Opry), Cleda and Jimmy Driftwood (country music balladeer), and Iron Eyes Cody whom I was pleased to assist once again. Iron Eyes received a Little Red River and Greers Ferry Hall of Fame Award for his participation and good example.

Keep America Beautiful Week and and National Litterbag Day calls full attention to the necessity of joining together to fight litter. A convenient way to Keep America Beautiful is USE A LITTER BAG!

The Noteworthy Company of Amsterdam, N.Y., under the leadership of Tom Constantino as president, is the leading manufacturer of litter bags, promoting their use with proper slogans and personal-

An advertisement used by the Noteworthy Company. From left: Woodsy Owl, Iron Eyes, Tom Constantino (President of Noteworthy), Smokey Bear, and McGruff, The Crime Prevention Dog. Photo by John Conboy, 1984.

ized advertising. Noteworthy does the printing of the beautiful posters, postcards, etc. of Iron Eyes, and has published some of his books. While working hand in hand with Keep America Beautiful, this company recently did a book about Iron Eyes called CHILDREN OF THE WORLD as a fund raiser for some worthwhile causes.

The annual Keep America Beautiful National Awards Luncheon, hosted by Roger Powers, President, features KAB awards to individuals, civic groups media, government agencies, schools, communities, and corporations whose leadership the past year reflect the finest in community improvements. Good words from high places came in 1982 when President Ronald Reagan, invited as a major speaker, cited the Clean Community System as "the type of positive, voluntary citizen action that this Administration supports." Iron Eyes has been honored for eighteen years of service in Keep America Beautiful. As he puts it, "I'm going on nineteen years."

As National Spokesman for Keep America Beautiful, Iron Eyes visits many states throughout the nation each year, talking to community organizations and youth groups, emphasizing the significance of anti-litter practices. He has special appeal to children; they understand his sadness and want to help him in the struggle. It is important to teach the children by letting them be a physical part of the cleanup. After a child has helped to pick up litter, he will think twice before throwing it out. Anti-litter children become anti-litter adults.

People make a personal commitment to Keep America Beautiful; the deepest of which produces the standards by which we strive to respect the rights of all to have a clean land. We must rely upon voluntary response and self-will to achieve the goals of clean cities, parks, and communities. And don't forget the roads that lead there because that is the first image that visitors see. Adopt a specific area and clean it up; begin small and keep branching out.

Our Indian ancestors did not pollute the land. Every part of an animal was eaten or used for clothing, lodging, etc. They had to drink and bathe in the lake, so they sure didn't throw things in it.

Many moons ago when I first began

The postcard was printed by The Noteworthy Company. The painting was done by John Steele.

to assist Iron Eyes, we were at a dinner meeting preceding a cleanup project. He introduced me and asked me to stand. Instead of standing, I just raised my hand, and he said, "Another shy girl."

The truth is, I would rather listen to his voice than my own. And when I stand up, I'm apt to start talking about my two favorite subjects, Iron Eyes Cody and Arkansas. Then it's hard to shut me up.

Everywhere I go, people soon learn that I'm from Arkansas, the natural state, and I'm proud of Arkansas. I'm also proud of my friend, Iron Eyes, who so well presents and represents our American heritage and the right to a naturally clean environment. If we all pull together to clean up the litter that's out there, then strive to personally live cleaner lives, we will see a more beautiful America.

Nothing in the drama of motion pictures, as much as I love movies, can equal the emotion I feel when I see "that tear." I can't imagine what America would have missed had he not been put here on this earth. It is my desire to be a part of whatever it takes to someday wipe the tear from the face of Iron Eyes Cody.

New address for Keep America Beautiful: 9 West Broad Street, Stamford, Connecticut 06902.

When he was hardly more than a child himself, Iron Eyes helped the small ones. In the 1920's and 1930's, while he was in foreign countries with the wild west shows, he spent his extra time at hospitals, visiting the children, telling stories, playing games, and entertaining with dances in places where he didn't even know the language.

,Like cowboys Gene Autry and Roy Rogers, Iron Eyes had his own line of wearing apparel for youngsters. Iron Eyes Enterprises incorporated February 7, 1952, with a full line of Indian clothing designed by Iron Eyes: breach cloths, moccasins, arm bands, jackets, boy suits, girl dresses, one-feather "Brave" bands, three-feather bucktail for "Warriors," and "Chief" war bonnets. T-shirts carried his name and picture. These were sold in stores along with those of Hopalong Cassidy and Annie Oakley, to cover the full range of cow-boys, cowgirls and Indians.

There is heritage in wisdom, making education a precious commodity. Children, love, education, future -- these words are

Iron Eyes Indian apparel for children, 1952.

synonymous with Iron Eyes. The future lies with the children who need love and education to reach their full potential in body, mind and spirit.

Iron Eyes' words to children contain messages of anti-smoking, anti-alcohol-use and anti-drug use. He tells them not to be afraid to say NO to an offer of drugs or NO to a daredevil feat. Just because someone is called "chicken," it isn't ne-cessary to do foolish things. Bravery should be saved for something good and special, so the person will be remembered as wise.

Iron Eyes is an optimist and children feel it when near him as he sings Indian songs that he learned as a boy. The chil-dren learn that Iron Eyes believes in books and that he is on the Board of Directors of the Los Angeles County Library. He encourages them to do their best, to take part in the betterment of their personal lives, their families, homes, schools and communities.

Iron Eyes feels that children should be taught spiritual values in life with the blending of the safekeeping of people,

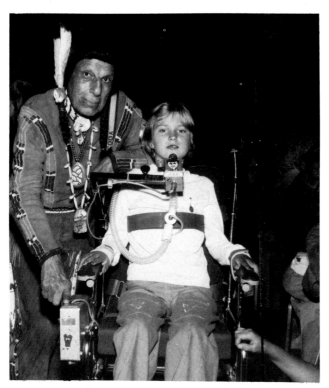

Iron Eyes encouraging the handicapped.

animals and earth. To accept nature's way and to care for the needs of each other is very important to a person's own feeling of inner worth.

Positive thinking can help to overcome pain and give strength where needed. A working faith in The Great Spirit, God, helps us to accept what comes that we do not understand; faith holds us together when we might otherwise fall apart.

One must go the extra mile in all undertakings; one person is as good as another. All people should enjoy themselves, have fun being together, and be satisfied within when one finds himself alone. Put service to others ahead of your own wants and do it with a pleasant, happy face.

All this is Iron Eyes' philosophy to children. When he tells them about himself, they like hearing how he rode his horse bareback to school. The legends he tells makes them proud to have Indian heritage, or proud to know someone of Indian heritage.

Iron Eyes spends much of his time in personal appearances with the monetary

Jamboree of fifty thousand scouts at Irvin Ranch, California, July 19, 1953. Roy Rogers was around there somewhere.

rewards going to various children's organizations. He helps support the Hope Ranch for needy children in Popular, Montana, and is helping Ben Johnson found and fund a spastic school in California.

Along with blood-brother Jock O'Mahoney, Iron Eyes helped man the telephones when the Marines joined with the Stars to promote Toys for Tots for twelve hours over radio and TV.

There is no way to estimate the value of years of service that Iron Eyes has devoted to the Boy Scouts, the teaching of sign language, photography, etc. Both of his sons are Eagle Scouts; Iron Eyes himself is a vigil member of the Order of the Arrow. He brings excitement to the Boy Scout Jamborees with his Indian costumes, dances and drums. The year 1987 marked the 77th Anniversary of the Boy Scouts of America; Iron Eyes has been honored for 45 years of service to this fine organization.

In the Pride Clubs of America, Iron Eyes has served as National Chairman, and

Birdie, Robert, and Iron Eyes. Robert is wearing the Iron Eyes Indian apparel.

is currently a Director, along with A & M Recording stars, George and Lewis Johnson (the Brothers Johnson); singer-songwriter, Virgil Beckham; and founder, Don Drowty.

Pride Clubs began in 1977 when Santa Monica school teacher, Don Drowty helped a group of students to join together to clean up the school grounds and surrounding area. They extended it into voluntarily assisting the handicapped and those in nursing homes.

After being in service only one year, the Pride Club received a Presidential Award as the top environmental service club in the United States. Now with the help of Optimist International, Sunrise Optimists Club, and the Santa Monica-Malibu Board of Education, Pride Clubs are springing up elsewhere. Children are standing up for conservation and preservation; they have the opportunity to learn how meaningful it is to help others.

Through the Don Drowty Youth Foundation, volunteers of all ages provide wheelchairs, crutches, clothes, shoes, medical supplies, educational material, art supplies and so much more to over 20,000 children in 27 states, Canada and Mexico.

The co-founders of A & M Records, Herb Albert and Jerry Moss, and their constituents are dedicated to the project. Iron Eyes is understandably proud of his involvement in the work of Pride Clubs and the Don Drowty Foundation.

Iron Eyes as YMCA Camp Indian Guide 1958. Robert Cody is in center with Arthur Cody next to Iron Eyes. Photo by Larry Harmon.

Iron Eyes in Fort Wayne, Indiana, 1975.

For information on how to start your own Pride Club, write to: Junior Optimists Pride Clubs of the Americas, P.O. Box 488, Santa Monica, CA 90406, or to Don Drowty Youth Foundation, P.O. Box 878, Paradise, CA 95969.

A wise Indian named Iron Eyes said: "I let children talk. You can't fool 'em. A child gets straight to the subject and stays there with questions and need for knowledge. We could learn much from them. Kids can influence the adults, their parents, to improve themselves, to kick bad habits like smoking, drinking and drugs."

Children are like a rainbow, all colors beautiful. Is it any wonder that all children love Iron Eyes?

"Daddy, can I be a chief someday?" Iron Eyes and son, Robert.

Walt Disney with Arthur, Robert, and Iron Eyes Cody.

During the lifetime of Iron Eyes, the United States has had thirteen presidents, most of whom he has been privileged to know. Though he never met Woodrow Wilson or Warren G. Harding, he did see Calvin Coolidge once on a train when a group of Indians shared the same passenger car. Same for Herbert Hoover, on a train. It was during Hoover's term that the Veterans Administration was created in 1930.

Beginning with Franklin D. Roosevelt, Iron Eyes has been good friends with all of the Presidents. Roosevelt, who had contracted poliomyelitis, came in a wheelchair to the Hollywood Bowl where Iron Eyes danced for him and then pushed him around in the wheelchair. A picture was taken but Longplume, Iron's father, lost it. During an invited visit to Washington, D.C., Roosevelt was in the first car of the parade; Iron Eyes was in the second. When a tree limb fell right on the President's car, it stopped the parade which was moving slowly anyway because of the tanks. Iron Eyes jumped out and got that limb and took the seeds from it home with him to Los Angeles. The pods were boiled so it would germinate. That pepper tree is still growing in his back yard and sometimes nearly covers the house.

Throughout World War II, Iron Eyes worked as an undercover agent, a shipyard welder for the FBI. With a sparkle in his eye, he recalls, "I was a spy!" He also served as an Air Raid Warden and was a member of The Code Talkers.

Upon the death of Roosevelt in 1945, Vice President Harry S. Truman took the reins; he didn't even know that the U.S. had a workable atom bomb because in those days the Vice President was kept in the dark.

Harry Truman liked Indian dances and Iron Eyes was to dance for him when the Presidential Train arrived in Los Angeles. However, the President got busy inside the train and missed the outside performance; so he shouted to Iron Eyes, as the train pulled away, "I'll see you in Washington." Upon special request, Iron Eyes danced for Truman in the White House. From then on, whenever the two met, the first thing Truman would say was, "Will you dance?" Truman was liked for his down-to-earth, tell-it-like-it-is way of getting his point across.

While Iron Eyes was on a trip into Colorado with Colonel Tim McCoy (movie cowboy star and friend to the Indian), it was learned that President Dwight D. Eisenhower was hospitalized in Denver. Upon their arrival at the hospital, they found him outside greeting people. When Iron Eyes walked within eyesight, Ike waved at him. They had been introduced previously by General George Patton.

In 1953, when Earl Warren was appointed by Eisenhower as the 14th Chief Justice, Iron Eyes was invited by both of them for the occasion.

Iron Eyes met John F. Kennedy while in the service in World War II. Kennedy was a happy person and was liked instantly. When the time came, Iron Eyes readily campaigned for the youngest president ever elected (at age 43). Kennedy gave him a two-headed coin as a sign of friendship.

Iron Eyes visited Kennedy at the White House concerning "Save the Eagle." This visit resulted in new and stiffer laws and restraints on killing eagles.

John F. Kennedy authored some manuscripts about the Great Indian History of the Plains Indians. Some of his histories were used in the TV series GREAT ADVENTURES that Iron Eyes did with Joseph Cotten.

When Kennedy was killed in 1963, Lyndon Baines Johnson acceded to The Presidency. He appointed the above mentioned Chief Justice, Earl Warren to head the committee to investigate the assassination; the Warren Commission Report was issued in 1964. Medicare was signed into law by Johnson in 1965. These programs have been helpful to the Indian people.

The best bar-b-que that Iron Eyes ever ate was at Lyndon Baines Johnson's Ranch in Texas. President Johnson, quite a comedian, would slip around and spike the punch. If anyone caught him at it, he would start speaking fluent Mexican. Mrs. Johnson asked Iron Eyes to represent her with Keep Texas Beautiful, after which, she recommended him for Keep America Beautiful.

The home of Richard M. Nixon is a good place for Iron Eyes to have nice,

78

Stonewall, Texas

April 28, 1987

Dear Ms. Thompson,

How pleased I am that you and Iron Eyes Cody are doing a book about his life!

The poignancy of his participation in the Keep America Beautiful campaign has helped to instill in our nation the will and the need to preserve all that is precious to us. He has performed a great service for us, and I am proud to be one of his fellow workers in the beautification 'vineyard'.

Sincerely,

Lady Bird Johnson

Ms. Marietta Thompson
Route 1, Box 114
Tuckerman, Arkansas 72473

CTJ:BT

quiet visits with him. Any time Former President Nixon is in the hospital, he can expect a visit from this nation's foremost Indian. Nixon is a well-liked gentleman who believes that all people should have the opportunity to be educated. The unfortunate Watergate incident cost the United States, as many people believe, one of our greatest presidents.

President Gerald R. Ford made good, careful selections when he appointed new members to the National Advisory Council on Indian Education. Ford is a great sportsman whom Iron Eyes meets on the golf course. He believes in taking care of the sick and supports his wife in the founding of the Betty Ford Clinic. Ford made every effort to uphold the good name of the Office of the Presidency.

Iron Eyes had a vision that Jimmy Carter would win his election. Iron even announced the vision to a thousand Indians at National Indian Day. He had known Carter as governor of Georgia, and Iron Eyes campaigned for the Carter-Mondale ticket.

On April 22, 1978, to launch a year of celebration commemorating the 25th Anniversary of Keep America Beautiful, President Carter was visited by the distinguished Indian, Iron Eyes Cody, who bestowed upon him the name "Wamblee Ska" (Great White Eagle), and presented Carter with an Eagle Feather Headdress which made the news nationwide. The headdress was a little small, and the pressure on his head must have confused The President, because when asked how to spell "Amy" so that Iron Eyes could sign a poster for her, The President said, "A-M-I-E or is it A-M-Y?" Carter was a good sport! He laughed and shook hands with Iron Eyes.

Twice Iron Eyes accompanied Carter to Rome, Italy. The first was a twelve day trip to discuss the hostage situation with The Pope. The hostages were released on the tenth day, the same day that the book IRON EYES, MY LIFE AS A HOLLYWOOD INDIAN was released. The second trip was for the beatification of Kateri Tekakwitha.

President Carter is a scholar and a gentleman; Iron Eyes enjoys visiting with the whole family.

On January 20, 1981, riding in President Ronald Reagan's Inaugural Parade was friend and Indian Grand Marshal, Iron Eyes

THE WHITE HOUSE
WASHINGTON

April 27, 1978

To Iron Eyes Cody

It was a special pleasure to welcome you to the White House recently, and I was pleased to have the opportunity to join you in marking "Keep America Beautiful Day."

Thank you for the headdress which you handcrafted and for bestowing your name, "White Eagle," upon me. You may be sure I will always treasure these honors as reminders of your friendship and goodwill.

Sincerely,

Jimmy Carter

Mr. Iron Eyes Cody
2999 West Sixth Street
Los Angeles, California 90020

Pope John Paul II and Iron Eyes in Rome, Italy, 1980.

dent when he closed his speech with: "As the President of the United States and as a Christian, I present to you, His Holiness, Pope John Paul II."

Then the Holy Father congratulated the Indians for giving the church Kateri and spoke of freedom for all people. When he closed, he whispered, "God Bless America."

Our United States people had gifts for the Pope; but how were they going to get to him with these gifts? There were such crowds and many guards. As the Pope and the President turned to leave, Iron Eyes called out, "Mr. President." And the President gave recognition and called back, "Iron Eyes." This allowed the opportunity to approach them and present to the Pope and President the pictures

from Tom Constantino that John Steele had painted of Kateri, using a picture of Birdie Cody as model.

Iron Eyes told the Pope there were other gifts for him, including a likeness of the Pope surrounded by the children of many nations. His Holiness expressed his appreciation of the beauty of the gifts from a beautifully varied group of people.

Sunday, June 22, was the day of beatification. This time there were seats. The program contained ninety-four pages of prayers and rituals.

During the ceremonies, His Holiness read the formula for beatification and assigned a day of feast for Kateri, April 17. She had died and entered into the glory on that date in history; so it seemed a fitting date to remember her.

There was much singing of hymns. The gospel presented was built around the scripture: "You are the salt of the earth. You are the light of the world." There was hardly a dry eye in the place when all the people of the world, different tongues and cultures, all recited the profession of faith together: "We believe in one God, the Father, the Almighty, maker of heaven and earth, of all that is seen and unseen. We believe in one Lord, Jesus Christ, the only Son of God..."

Another day the Pope held a special audience with the Indians and representatives of Canada and the United States. Security was heavy. Tom Constantino, who was unknown to the guards, was stopped for identification. Up walked Iron Eyes and proclaimed: "He's my brother. He goes!" And that was the end of that because they all knew who Iron Eyes was.

The following is an excerpt from His Holiness' address to these pilgrim Indians: "You have made this long journey to Rome to participate in a special moment in the history of your people. You have come to rejoice in the beatification of Kateri Tekakwitha. It is a time to pause and to give thanks to God for the unique culture and rich human tradition which you have inherited, and for the greatest gift anyone can receive, the gift of faith. Indeed, Blessed Kateri stands before us as a symbol of the best of the heritage that is yours as North American Indians."

It was Pope John Paul II who told Iron Eyes to go visit the Basilica of St. Francis of Assisi, Patron of Ecology. When Iron Eyes saw the likeness of the Saint who cried, he knew from where the idea for the tear in the Keep America Beautiful commercials came.

Those who looked upon His Holiness would probably agree with Iron Eyes who suggested that a good Indian name for the Pope would be "Talking Eyes," for he speaks with his eyes before he has even uttered a word.

CHAPTER 6

GIFTS TO FUTURE GENERATIONS

One of the finest legacies that can be left to future generations is a knowledge of heritage, language, customs, traditions, legends, ideas, feelings and remembrances of our ancestors. With a desire to participate in the homecoming reunions of powwows and dancing, we need a place to observe blessed items of the long-ago time.

The Moosehead Museum, owned by Iron Eyes, and in the basement of his Los Angeles home, is one of the finest private collections of Indian artifacts and relics in the world. This collection began with Iron Eyes' father and has been used extensively by studios. The masks, paintings, and enviable regalia have provided authenticity to many movies over the years. This extensive library on the American Indian is not only a source of pride but also a wealth of available knowledge.

Iron Eyes and his wife, Birdie, worked together to add important items: the war bonnet of Sitting Bull, moccasins of Two Gun White Calf, a three thousand year old pipe, one of very few Apache

Iron Eyes, Birdie, Arthur, and Robert in their own Moosehead Museum.

84

violins, a buffalo hide painted to tell the story of Wounded Knee. Medicine Man, Francis Sweetwater, blessed a tiny beaded bag of holy peyote and placed it among the plethora of beautiful war bonnets, beaded buckskins, belts, mocassins, leggings, pelts, drums, bows and arrows.

The Codys were close friends with Maria Martinis, a great lady potter who lived until 1982, and contributed much to the making and preservation of Indian pottery. Items about her have been written in history books. In addition to articles of her original work presented to the Codys, she helped to identify many pieces of pottery that Birdie unearthed in her diggings.

There's no way to estimate how many people have visited and received benefit from the Moosehead Museum which began with the collections of Longplume Cody. In order to preserve it so that millions may continue to enjoy it, Iron Eyes has decided to place his items in various larger museums.

In addition to the items entrusted to Gene Autry, 120 pieces of Iron Eyes' collection are at Roy Rogers' museum in Victorville, CA. Donations were given to the Cowboy Hall of Fame in Oklahoma City, OK and to Friends of William S. Hart (silent movie cowboy) Park in Newhall, CA.

Visitor, Los Angeles Chief of Police, Ed Davis, looking at the true pipestone pipe in 1977. Chief Davis won the office of U.S. Senator after Iron Eyes smoked the blessed pipe for him. As a gift Iron Eyes then gave him the pipe.

The Turtle Museum near Niagara Falls, N.Y. houses all sorts of paraphernalia associated with the Turtle Clan of the Iroquois to which Birdie Cody belonged. Among other things given was a portion of Birdie's jewelry, twenty-five silver brooches.

Birdie left four beaded necklaces for four people who appreciate and understand the Indians' need and way of life: Lillian Gish, Connie Stevens, Sandy Redhawk; and I have the fourth. I proudly wear the red, white, and yellow beads of early Apache design. Birdie was wonderful with tiny beads and designs of various tribes. She made numerous pieces for Iron Eyes that he wears on special occasions.

The Southwest Museum in Los Angeles shares the protection of many of Birdie's findings. Iron Eyes is proud to be affiliated with an institution that repre-

Visitor, Christopher Lee (Dracula) examining the bonnet of Sitting Bull.

Iroquoian collection. Notice the two turtle shells representative of Birdie's clan, the Turtle Clan of the Seneca Tribe of Iroquois.

sents our people with dignity. He serves as a member of the Board of Trustees.

In 1948 the Moosehead Museum was the gathering place for a famous group of Indians: the survivors and sons of survivors who actually fought in the Battle of Little Big Horn in 1876. They had come to Los Angeles to be on a TV show. They were all old, but they made big medicine that day. They had a great Uwipi Ceremonial Feast and discussed what really happened to "Yellow Hair" (General George Custer).

Among the group was John Sitting Bull, son of the famous Sioux Medicine Man, Sitting Bull. John, age 92, having been deaf since age 2, spoke in sign language. That was a day of high honor for the Moosehead Museum and its owners.

Iron Eyes and Birdie with one of the artifacts of elaborate design that she discovered in 1930. Photo by Eddie Hoff.

Home to the Indian has always been a place of rest, ease, and peace. Shelters were needed in extremely cold weather; but the rest of the time, the outdoors was home -- anywhere there was water, grass for horses, shade for summer, and pure fresh air to breathe. Was there ever a more beautiful ceiling than a sky full of stars, clouds, sun, and moon?

Indians are the most resourceful people on earth. They've shown an ability to deal promptly and effectively with difficulties. Should they show any less strength in the use of raw materials for shelter?

Contrary to common belief, not all Indians lived in tepees or wigwams; and incidentally, tepees and wigwams are not the same thing. Simply, tepees are pole framed, cone-like, and covered with skins. Wigwams have a frame of arched poles, are dome-shaped, and are covered with bark. Builders varied the shapes and coverings to whatever was available.

Tepee in backyard, 1953. In case wife put Iron Eyes in "Doghouse." Iron Eyes made the Double Trailer Headdress with 101 eagle feathers; Birdie made the beaded headband. This tepee belonged to the Cody children.

Where there was no proper bark or skins, shelters could be formed by putting up a frame of poles in a beehive shape with bunches of grass tied to it. In winter, dirt could be heaped on.

A hogan was built by surrounding a set of poles with another set of poles and filling the space between with mud and bark.

Some tribes had rectangular houses made of planks split from cedar logs. Posts were set, and the planks were tied to them with vines. Walls might be mud plastered and roofs could be thatched. Others built earth lodges, partly underground, covered with logs and dirt.

Among the most unique structures were the four and five stories high, great terraced adobehouses built by the Pueblo.

An Indian's home even back in the days of tepees, was his own, to be not only his shelter, but a place for displaying his accomplishments, whether meager or great.

Iron Eyes' home was no exception; but since the awards and accomplishments of nearly eight decades have accumulated, the wall space has run out and the layers of memorabilia have stacked up. He is seldom home, but each time he returns, he adds the latest to the top of the layers. As a widower of some ten years, housekeeping is at a minimum and often there is only a pathway, but it is like entering a collector's dream.

The first time I was there, I couldn't believe my eyes; and time would not allow me in four days to read and learn all that I had hoped to. Several visits later, I am still amazed at finding things completely overlooked previously. Iron Eyes says I have a way of finding items he has searched for for years or had forgotten completely.

While Iron Eyes could have purchased a larger and finer home, as many of his Star friends have done, he chooses to remain in the place where his heart is, where his father resided, where Iron Eyes and Birdie lived and raised their children.

The unpretentious, white stucco home in an older section of the Hollywood Hills, is situated in an area that was once the filming ground for countless movies. It

Iron Eyes in his office-den. Painting on wall of Birdie and Iron Eyes by Kathryn Leighton.

was originally the office of D. W. Griffith when BIRTH OF A NATION was being filmed in 1915. Longplume (Iron Eyes' father) bought the place and with the help of Tohamid Darkcloud (Birdie's grandfather), constructed additions. The nearby park was named Griffith Park (where Gene Autry's Western Heritage Museum is), and the street in front of the house is Griffith Park Boulevard.

In 1964, the week of July 18-24, TV Guide carried an article by Leslie Raddatz on Iron Eyes entitled "Him Hollywood Indian," in which reference is made to his living quarters. As a bit of fun, the following is excerpted:

"... Of course, Iron Eyes good at sign language, especially dollar sign. Him have nice tepee in Hollywood, with big yellow Cadillac out back in little tepee for wagon-that-run-without-horse.

"Nothing like that in Texas or Oklahoma when Iron Eyes a papoose. That almost 50 winters ago, him say. Iron Eyes tells how him come to Hollywood in 1921. That means him only 7 years old then – and before that work on banana boat to Mexico and tour U.S. and Canada with 101 Wild West Show... Either Iron Eyes forget a few winters, or else him plenty precocious papoose.

"Iron Eyes do first acting for DeMille in UNCONQUERED. Play Indian Chief, chase Paulette Goddard all through picture. Never catch Paulette, but in 1934 marry pretty Seneca Indian maid, Ye-Was. Then right away Iron Eyes go to Australia for two years, leave Ye-Was in Los Angeles. In Australia, Iron Eyes shoot 21 kangaroo with bow and arrow. In Los Angeles, Ye-Was feel like shooting Iron Eyes. Her archeologist... at Southwest Museum in Los Angeles... Now she and Iron Eyes have own museum in basement of split-level Hollywood tepee.."

Anywhere an Indian lives there will be something to represent the eagle or its feathers. The eagle is held in high esteem

Enviable war bonnet on a young Iron Eyes, age 12.

as the symbol of freedom and bravery. Even a single feather signifies power.

In the U.S. the eagle has been protected by a migratory treaty act since 1940. Indians are the only people who can legally have eagle feathers and can get them from the government because of the ceremonial significance involved. Indians can swap or give the feathers but cannot sell them.

During an Indian ceremonial dance if someone accidentally drops an eagle feather, by custom it cannot be picked up, except by a wounded war veteran who dances in a respectful ceremonial dance around the fallen feather. He reaches down for it and as he picks it up, the music stops. He carries it to its owner who must thank him and present him with a gift for his thoughtfulness. Even a feather itself is a fine acceptable offering for the return.

White men often do not understand the importance of a single feather, but with knowledge the meaning becomes clearer. A feather is an outward show of honor. The right to wear it must be earned in some way. For instance, a feather split lengthwise up the shaft and spread into two forks is like a medal to a badly wounded veteran.

Feathers can be earned by foolhardy courage, called "counting coup," by striking

Iron Eyes is wearing in 1937, an Eagle Feather, Ermine, Buffalo Head Piece that was given to the Moosehead Museum by Tim McCoy who obtained it in 1914.

On the set of a Shirley Temple movie SUSANNAH OF THE MOUNTIES, 1939, a variety of eagle feather war bonnets from Iron Eyes' collection. Photo taken by Iron Eyes.

an armed enemy with one's bare hand or stick, for disarming an enemy, for stealing a horse from an enemy's camp without being detected, etc.

Various cuts into the feathers have various meanings of the particular deeds performed; the tip cut diagonally signifies that an enemy's throat has been cut. Feathers can be read the same as a book can be read. If a plain eagle feather is worn horizontally in the hair, coup has counted in some way, and the wearer can marry before the age of 25; no feather, no marriage.

Each coup feather had the makings of a great story to be told. Sometimes the stories were saved along with the feathers until there were enough for a war bonnet. Friends were invited to feast, smoke the pipe, and make a bonnet while listening to the tale of the deed performed for each feather. This makes for a nice social ceremony as the feathers are sorted and laid out according to size and degree of bravery.

If a warrior earned more coup feathers than needed for a full-size headdress, he was allowed to make a bonnet that had eagle feathers hanging down the back in single or double-row fashion. Only the bravest and most daresome had the double trailer war bonnets.

Arkansas now has the best record for protection of eagles after having had the worst record some years ago; the way is being changed. There is a $5,000 fine and one year in jail imposed by the state and $20,000 fine and one year in jail by federal law for killing a Bald Eagle, our national symbol. A sizeable population of eagles is found in Arkansas from October to March when eagles follow the flight of the ducks.

The Pawnee tribe teaches the children lessons in life with a legend about the eagle feather, simplified here:

The eagle was the most loved by The Great Spirit for it tells the story of life. The eagle has two eggs, as all living things are divided into two: man and woman, male and female, as it is with animals, birds, trees and flowers. All things have children of two kinds so that life may continue.

Man has two eyes, two hands, two feet, body and soul. Through his eyes he sees pleasant and unpleasant scenes. Through his nostrils he smells good and bad odors. With his ears he hears joyful noise and sad news. His mind is divided between good and evil. His right hand may do evil, but his left hand which is near his heart, is full of kindness. His right foot may lead him to the wrong path, but his left foot always pulls him the correct way.

To remember the lessons of life, look to the eagle. The eagle feather is divided into two parts, light and dark, representing daylight and darkness, or summer and winter, peace and war, life and death.

When confused, breathe a prayer on the eagle's pure white down and send it upward to The Great Spirit.

The right to wear the eagle's feather is earned by an act of valor. It is to be

Making an eagle feather headdress at MGM Studio in 1940.

90

worn with dignity and pride; and through it to always remember the story of life.

Instead of "Once upon a time," an Indian story would likely begin with "Many moons ago." In the days long past, Indian folklore was preserved as myths and legends when the birds and animals walked and talked. It was handed down from parent to child, and grandparent to grandchild. The stories told of the creation of the world, storms, and other happenings of nature, how each animal got its features, of spirits and ancestors departed, and of the adventures of men.

All Indian tribes had poetry. It did not rhyme, but more resembled free verse with lines of all different lengths. Poems were used to tell a tribe's history, to express emotion, for hymns and prayers, war ceremonies, magic rites, or a lesson

Iron Eyes painting a friend's Seminole drum in 1964. The base was over 100 years old.

taught. Most of the poetry was sung as songs, but there was no harmony; all voices sang the melody.

During the 1800's a famous poet, Henry Wadsworth Longfellow wrote about an Indian hero by the name of Hiawatha. All people should read his work for the lessons that can be learned from it. A lesson about bragging is learned in a quote from the epic poem THE SONG OF HIAWATHA, about an Indian named Iagoo:

And Iagoo, the great boaster,
He the marvelous story-teller,
He the friend of old Nokomis,
Jealous of the sweet musician,
Jealous of the applause they gave him
Saw in all the eyes around him,
Saw in all their looks and gestures,
That the wedding guests assembled
Longed to hear his pleasant stories,
His immeasurable falsehoods.
Very boastful was Iagoo;
Never heard he an adventure
But himself had met a greater;
Never any deed of daring
But himself had done a bolder;
Never any marvelous story
But himself could tell a stranger.
Would you listen to his boasting,
Would you only give him credence,
No one ever shot an arrow
Half so far and high as he had;
Ever caught so many fishes,
Ever killed so many reindeer,
Ever trapped so many beaver!
None could run so fast as he could,
None could dive so deep as he could,
None could swim so far as he could;
None had made so many journeys,
None had seen so many wonders,
As this wonderful Iagoo,
As this marvelous story-teller!
Thus his name became a by-word
And a jest among the people;
And whene'er a boastful hunter
Praised his own address too highly,
Or a warrior, home returning,
Talked too much of his achievements,
All his hearers cried, "Iagoo!
Here's Iagoo come among us!"

Music was played on handmade instruments, the drum being the most highly regarded and recognized. There were many kinds of drums. Some were like the tambourines with a hide stretched on one side of a frame; others had two sides as we think of a modern drum. Panpipes were reeds of various lengths tied together. Flutes were made of bone or cane. Trumpets were made from gourds and shells. Gourds with pebbles placed inside became rattles. Castanets were formed by bunching together small objects that rattled: bird beaks, deer hoofs or cocoons. Anything that made a sound could be a musical instrument if held by a skilled tribesman.

Speaking of a skilled tribesman, in Burbank, California lives a young Creek man, Alexander Longrifle. He is a talented singer, musician, and songwriter. He records for Pinto Records somewhat in the style of Elvis Presley. On his album, SILVER EAGLE is an appropriate song he wrote. Alex is a close friend and it is with pride in his work that we include the words of that song:

IRON EYES CODY

He's a symbol of the plight
   of the Indian man.
For he has cried for he has seen the
   destruction of his ancestors' land.
Cherokee Man, you've done your best
   for us all.
Iron Eyes, like legend you walk tall,
   Changing the wind,
   Moving with the times.

Freedom of Eagles.
Wisdom from men.
He's walked with the Presidents,
Humbled with all of them.

Future generations may read
   about this man.
May regret the times they didn't
   listen, or understand.
Fighting pollution, you've done your
   best for the American land.
Iron Eyes, like legend you walk tall,
   Changing the wind,
   Moving with the times.

Freedom of Eagles.
Wisdom from men.
He's walked with the Presidents,
Humbled with all of them.

As a child, Iron Eyes was known as Little Eagle, one who was light on his feet

as a dancer, and one who endured all things well. He was being watched by White Horse, the great Arapaho Chief, who decided that Little Eagle was growing up and needed a man's name. White Horse had once known a great chief by the name of Iron Eyes, who had strong endurance. Iron Eyes (Ista Maza in Arapaho) would be a good name for Little Eagle.

Chief White Horse invited important Indians to come to a feast and ceremony: Big Tree, Red Thunder, White Feather, Shave Head, Silvermoon, Chief Yowlachie, Flying Bear, Running Deer, Willowbird, Weasel Tail, Standing Bear, Chief Goes-in-Lodge, White Bird, Walks Alone, and many others.

Colonel Tim McCoy was also among the invited guests; he sang, danced, and

Champion Dancer Iron Eyes demonstrated both archery and dancing at the 1932 Olympics. Costume was made by IEC. This was the year that Buster Crabbe won a gold medal for 400 meter freestyle.

Painting of Iron Eyes by Kathryn W. Leighton of his participation in 1932 Olympics.

told wonderful stories of adventure.

Chief White Horse gave a speech in Arapaho, talking about Little Eagle and the new name that had been selected. The Other Buffalo Dance was performed and Little Eagle became Iron Eyes.

As an added honor, because he now had an Arapaho name, the Arapaho Tribe adopted him; a fitting tribute. The ceremonial pipe of peace was passed around, with the smoke ascending upward to all ancestors to be witness to the new member of the Arapaho Tribe.

Now according to Indian custom, the one being honored must pay for all the expenses incurred during the feast and ceremony. How was Iron Eyes, so young, going to pay for all this? Wise friend, Tim McCoy came prepared, sponsored Iron Eyes, paid for it all, and would remain forever in the heart of Iron Eyes for his goodness and generosity. The generosity and unselfishness we find in Iron Eyes today is due in part to the influence of Colonel Tim McCoy.

As a teenager, Iron Eyes many times won the Junior Championship Fast Dance. He held the Senior Championship for four and a half years from 1941-45. In 1946, he came in second but continued to enter the contests until 1950 just to make the other contestants work harder to earn their winnings. Standing Bear Powwow participants took notice when they saw Iron Eyes

Iron Eyes in full dress dance outfit, 1942. Photo by Roland Allen.

enter the circle. He practically wore out all the judges!

Iron Eyes has talked to me often about my childhood. We swap stories, mine being somewhat lacking to his; but he has never stopped me yet in the middle of one. So here goes: Back when I was Chief of the Tribe (which consisted of my two young brothers), I wanted to impress them with my ability and know-how. On a dark day when I could look across the field and see a rain coming, I'd grab a band, tie it around my head, and shout as I ran out the door, "I'm goin'a do a rain dance!"

I'd start with the hoopla, jumping and dancing around. Soon the rain would move closer and I'd make a louder noise. By the time the rain was over us and I was getting soaked, the eyes of the little ones were as big as saucers. "How did you do that," they questioned. "You just have to know how," I'd answer. Then on a sunny day when they were playing outside, they'd try it for themselves, but it never rained. Guess they loved me in spite of all my ability.

Ready for any occasion, Iron Eyes' rain tale: In 1977, on the way to Palm Springs, for George Montgomery's Art Show, Iron Eyes stopped off at NBC-TV to do a special for John Sterns on a weather program. It started raining as Iron Eyes sang the Eagle Dance Song. It continued to rain all the way to Palm Springs, flooded all around the Desert Museum. It rained for three days and nearly ruined George's show! Guess George Montgomery believes in an Indian's ability to make rain!

Indian dancing today is representative of a past way of life and is a symbolic vision of the future. In discussing the dances, we may use both the past and present tense because it's nearly impossible to describe the present without feeling the past. So much of the past continues today in the hearts and minds of people of the Indian nations.

Dancing is most often a part of a ceremony of some sort; and most ceremonies are religious in nature. There are at least six occasions that are celebrated: The Maple Festival, The Planting, The Strawberry, The Green Corn, The Harvest, and The New Year. Most ceremonies concern food, praying for, being thankful for, and looking to the future to be good.

Indian dancing is not merely jumping up and down. There are intricate, very complicated routines. If it seems simple to the observer, then be advised that it's the skill of the dancer that makes it appear easy. It takes athletic ability, stamina, long endurance, and discipline of the limbs. The habitual activity of exertion lightens the work of the Medicine Man because his dancing people are healthier.

Dancing is an art; the dancer, an artist. There is unequalled beauty in the art of the dancer. All values the Indian possesses, life, ideal, the whole broad scope of his being and existence, is encompassed in the dance.

It has been said that blondes have more fun; but I think Indians have more fun. Some of the dancing is riotous. Each tribe performs any dance in its own particular way with similarities and differences from other tribes. Within a tribe, each dancer has his own individual style. Some dances are special to a particular tribe. I most enjoy an Inter-tribal dance where various tribes dance to the same beat, but each tribe does its own thing. The dances are decorative, light, heavy, dull, bright, cool, hot, slow, fast: all styles can be found.

While some routines are similar to others, the same dance may have more than one name; and one may be a take off from some other dance.

We'll attempt to show the variety in this sampling of dances. We won't try to fully describe them; but if this stirs your curiosity for further knowledge of a particular dance, then set out to learn. Begin with an inquiry of your elders, pleasurable for young and old. "Old One" might surprise you with a memorable demonstration. Then visit a library for good reading material.

If the opportunity presents itself, watch a young man, Phillip "Yoggi" Bread, a Kiowa-Cherokee, do his "grouse" dance. A treat is in store! Yoggi is one of the top rated dancers in the United States. He gave a brilliant performance while serving as Head Traditional Dancer for the 1986 Arkansas Powwow at Little Rock, held in conjunction with the state's sesqui-centennial celebration.

Also take notice of Donald Solomon, a teenager, Choctaw of the Mississippi Band, whose fancy feather and hoop dancing have won numerous competitions. Donald served proudly as Junior Boy Head Dancer at the same powwow.

The dances are part of the glorious and not so glorious past. They are kept in use as a way of preserving the custom of our heritage.

The GHOST DANCE has a certain place in history. The Basin type round dance included women, and was performed by many tribes, especially the Sioux and Arapaho. It began as a result of Christian mission influence among the Paviotso, a branch of Pah-Utes in Nevada.

In about 1880, an Indian named Jack "Wovoka" Wilson began to have visions, the result of which produced a new doctrine that combined Christian ethical ideas, that of a coming messiah, rituals to make the white man disappear, the dead Indians to reappear, and bring back the vanished buffalo. He forbade fighting and preached peace.

Word of his teaching reached the plains where people were desperate; starvation was everywhere. Here the doctrines took on a varied meaning which included war against the whites, with their own power magically fortified to become bullet proof. It was accepted as destiny. The dancing became endless with strange ferment, out of such great need for help.

The white men were so frightened of this dance that it led to the killing of Sitting Bull and to the Battle of Wounded Knee. Hunger has caused many wrongs.

In the GIVE-AWAY DANCE when a gift is given, one of like value must be given in return. When the return gift is received, it signifies that the feeling is mutual.

In the olden days when an Indian gave a white man a gift, and the white man failed to return a gift, the Indian was insulted and by custom had to ask for his gift to be given back. Thus, the white man's term "Indian giver" came from the lack of knowledge on the white man's part.

Anyone wishing to give a gift and re-ceive nothing in return must give the gift during a powwow-type dance and not a giveaway dance. Any newcomer, not knowledgeable as to which is which, should ask someone in authority.

The give-away dance is for the dancer's enjoyment with the giving and receiving of gifts as in the Christmas spirit.

The OTHER BUFFALO DANCE came about from the need for a young man to prove his manhood. A man's name should reflect something in particular about that man. Baby names are okay for babies and very young boys, but when a boy becomes a man, he must discard childish things and that includes his name.

A man's name is important; it should bear a good meaning; but it can be less than complimentary if the person's personality is so. A name is respected if it comes from the performance of a difficult deed.

The dance is named from the attempt to gain an important name. It seems a boy was anxious to prove himself; he pointed out the buffalo he would fell. He shot his arrow, and the buffalo went down; but just as he was about to claim the kill, up came another hunter and claimed it for himself. The second hunter proved it by ownership of the arrow in the buffalo.

Upon search, a second buffalo lay dead with the boy's arrow in it; his aim had been bad and he killed the wrong buffalo, the other buffalo. Thus came the name of the dance for the changing of the name, as it was when Iron Eyes' name was changed from Little Eagle.

The most challenging, fun dance is the PIPE DANCE, a powwow type solo. The attention is on the lone dancer who holds a pipe stem in one hand and a noise making rattle in the other. He bends forward as far as he can and tries to shape himself like a bowl of a pipe. The antics of the individual, the various body shapes, some overweight, make dancing bent over quite awkward, and causes laughter from the crowd.

To add to the ridicule, the drummers change tempo or rhythm without warning and cause the dancer to get out of time or jingle a rattle after the drum stops. When the performer has had all the ridicule he can stand, he looks for the one who has laughed the most, and presents the pipe stem to the person who must take his place in the dance area.

The challenge cannot be refused. All one can do is accept the pipe stem and get out there and try his best not to make a fool of himself.

The correct name for SNAKE DANCE is HOPI SNAKE DANCE, a ceremonial prayer which asks for rain so that crops will grow. The ritual is very quiet, intense, with snakes representing lightning, being blessed, and released to carry the prayer to the priests through the underground world up to heaven.

Snakes are gathered from the four directional points, known as the Four Winds, after which for nine days they are washed, prayed over, and purified in the kiva, a subterranean or partially subterranean chamber that can be entered only by a hole in the roof and the use of a ladder. The snakes are then brought out as brothers to participate in the dance.

The largest snake is selected, stroked until it becomes passive. A yellow feather is tied around its neck just before it is placed in a basket of cornmeal and carried to a valley dug on the west side. The priest makes a circle with more cornmeal on the ground and places the snake in the circle. The direction to which the snake glides away will be the direction from which the rain will come.

The Chief Snake Dancer goes to the Antelope Priest to receive instructions to invite the others to join in. The men form groups of three and only one will carry a snake in his mouth. The second man carries a snake-whip of feathers to use to distract the snake; the third man has to pick up the snake if it falls. It takes a year or more of preparation and study to become a snake dancer.

In the summers of 1935-37, Tim McCoy and Iron Eyes joined the Ringling Brothers and Barnum & Bailey Circus, and set up a wild west show. Iron Eyes hired a dozen Hopi Indians, snake dancers, and bought some five-foot rattlesnakes. He had the snakes defanged, but they still looked mighty mean to the audience.

Everything had to be as realistic as possible for Colonel Tim McCoy to allow his name to be used. J. W. "Silvermoon"

Cody designed all the authentic Hopi costumes.

Each year the show opened at Madison Square Garden in New York with Iron Eyes as Head Snake Dancer, even though he was the youngest of the group.

Spectators were kept spellbound with fear that a snake might bite one of the dancers, or worse yet, get loose in the crowd. Iron Eyes called the rattlesnakes "pets" and often one would die from too much tender, lovin' care.

The controversial SUN DANCE is a slow stomp, performed around a pole, set up in a circular space, enclosed by a token wall of brush. The dancers fast and drink no water in preparation of and during the dance. They must dance to exhaustion, faint, or have visions of benefit.

Self-torture was practiced by some tribes in the olden days and by some individuals not so long ago to demonstrate their hardiness and to cause more important dreams or visions to come.

In the movie A MAN CALLED HORSE, Iron Eyes portrayed The Sun Dance Priest, with a true account of the sacred sun dance ritual performed on

Iron Eyes and Jimmy Smith, Navajo, and snake friends, 1937.

96

Tim McCoy and wild west lineup – Ringling Bros. and Barnum & Bailey combined circus. Worcester, MA, June 25, 1937. Iron Eyes is fifth from left on back row. Photo by E. J. Kelty.

Richard Harris. It was a bit hard for the squeamish to watch, but authentic, none-theless.

For three years Iron Eyes participated in the Sun Dance of South Dakota, along with Bill Eagle Feather, Red Cloud, and Frank Foolscrow. After the process of purification in the sweat lodge, Iron Eyes joined the procession line. It was his duty to carry and present the all important buffalo skull to the Sun Dance Pole. He has been known to last out a three day ritual. How's that for endurance?

The War Dance was a stomp with menacing gestures by the performers, each using his own individuality. The dancers equipped themselves with war weapons such as tomahawks and shields. The purpose was to prepare for battle, to produce men ready for fighting -- warriors who felt stronger than they really were, and who were certain of successful endeavors.

One would give a war whoop and then the rest would respond with echo-sounding chorus. A war whoop was once described as a prolonged yell on a high note that slid downward and then started all over again.

Those of us who favor the "Cowboys and Indians" movies know that Iron Eyes has a terrific war whoop, a spine chilling yell that is unsurpassed. Undoubtedly, a recording of his yell must be among standardized equipment in the sound effects room of every major studio.

For a view of age-old dances, dis-plays of Indian culture, native crafts, Indian foods, rich heritage, and top-notch fellowship, one should attend the powwows that are scattered all over the U.S. at various times of the year. Some of the biggest and best are incorporated in what I call my district of participation: Arkansas, Tennessee and Mississippi, a great trio of states for my trio of interests (Indians, movie festivals and music).

Powwow is an Algonquian term, meaning "conjure" or "coming together." Originally when members of a hunting tribe were scattered, their common bond would bring them back together once or twice a year in reunion. The medicine man would perform ceremonies for healing, along with dancing and loud noise in thanks for a good hunt.

Native American religious ceremonies

are often held in conjunction with a pow-wow; it's hard to tell the difference. Nowadays even a type of dance is called a powwow; a style of dancing is called pow-wow dancing; and an evening of dancing is called a powwow. Among other things, it is a chance to whoop it up and have a good time, a social get-together.

The feasting, dancing, wailing chants, games, exotic sounds, muted thump of the tom-toms, the pulsating rhythm of the head drum, the non-stop drumming, the dancers' bells, singing voices, and applause combine to form the common denominator that links all Indians together.

Great distances are traveled to attend the gatherings that fulfill a need for restoration of the spirit. Harmony with nature and with the universe: sky, stars, trees, grass, dirt, and animals. This is the Indian's way of life. He needs it; he must have it. He needs the touch of the wind on his face, the silence of the heavens, the beauty of the night.

The urban Indian of today especially feels estranged from nature because of the concrete confines of work places and city residences. This separation from the past, distant way of life bears hard on him. His ties with mother nature are important and need renewing for the sake of inner worth. The urban Indian's needs are fulfilled with the powwows, the gathering of the clans and tribes.

What a sight! An Indian will bring out the traditional dress of his tribe, his ancestors: feathers, buckskins, leggings, beaded moccasins, fringe, sequined shawls, ribboned shirts, bells, rattles, the trimmings and decorations that best portray the past. He braids his hair. He is proud to paint his face or wear the roaches and headdress reminiscent of the long-ago time. Indians didn't paint their faces to look ferocious. The colors and lines represented visions or dreams they had had, a type of prediction of what was expected in life.

A powwow begins with the Grand Entry of dancers in full, resplendent dress, led by the head dancers. All people then stand for the flag song, followed with the invocation by a respected one. Each drum group may then sing a song, during which all sorts of dancing takes place, all keep-

ing step to the drum. Indians look to the heart of the individual and all are welcome.

To be entertained, watch dancers compete for excellence in a contest pow-wow with money prizes. They go all out for perfection in dress and movement. Contestants must register in proper categories prior to the Grand Entry, and are judged by experts from the audience. Between contests, there are social dances, again led by the head dancers. These dances are for everyone, including non-Indian people.

Vividly I remember a time when in Philadelphia, Mississippi, the head man dancer broke the circle, came out into the audience, and pulled me into the arena in the middle of a performance, to finish a dance with him, called "Changing Partners." I was hooked from then on. From the sideline, Iron Eyes was doing his own little dance, catching it all on camera.

Hundreds of costumed dancers can literally shake the foundations of buildings, so the most successful place to hold a powwow is always outdoors. Our ancestors lend spirit to the powwow and each person present begins to feel renewed inside. The religious aspect is greatly felt.

In connection with Arkansas' Sesquicentennial Celebration in June, 1986, the American Indian Center of Arkansas was host to an Inter-tribal Powwow, headed by Board Chairman, Edith Dalton. Special guests were Wilma Mankiller, the first woman Principal Chief of the Cherokee nation of Oklahoma, and our own Native American representative, Iron Eyes Cody. He gifted, presented, and dedicated to the center, a beautiful, much-needed ceremonial drum.

Master of Ceremonies was Sammy "Tonekei" White, Kiowa Tribe, of Oklahoma City, OK. A born leader, his voice has a soothing effect even when giving a command. The Great Spirit is with him. Those who live in the area that receives his weekly Indian TV show, TRIBES: VOICES FROM THE LAND, are truly blessed. Sammy was presented, with the help of Chief Wilma, the treasured Iron Eyes Cody Peace Medal.

When Iron Eyes introduced me to the gracious Chief Wilma, many happy mem-

98

ories went through my mind of "playing Indian" with my two younger brothers when I was ten years old and they were five and three. Even though I was a girl, I was oldest, biggest, and strongest; therefore, I was a woman chief long before women's lib reached the reservation or anywhere else for that matter. I tied bands around our heads and stuck in any kind of feathers I could find, usually chicken. I was affectionately known by the little ones as Big Chief Sis.

A typical conversation went something like this:

"Big Chief Sis, do you want to go on warpath today?"

"Maybe after the sun goes down, Brave Number One."

"But, Big Chief Sis, Indians don't go on the warpath at night."

"These Indians do, Brave Number Two, cause right now it's too hot outside."

"Then, Big Chief Sis, would you make us some Kool-Aid?"

"Okum-dokum."

For fifteen years, popular Master of Ceremonies, historian and lecturer, Iron Eyes Cody has graced the Philadelphia, Mississippi area with his presence at the Choctaw Indian Fair. Along with traditional activities, this particular powwow is combined with nightly entertainment by big name Nashville, Tennessee country music stars. Throngs of people converge there. A carnival with candy apples and cotton candy brings white man's world to the eyes of Indian children. Stick ball games are prevalent with the Mississippi Choctaws renown for their physical strength in the game.

The Choctow Indian reservation is one of the finest, cleanest, up to date, modern, financially functioning reservations in the United States. Paved streets, factories for greeting cards and automotive wiring have become reality among the long list of accomplishments of Chief Phillip Martin.

Chief Martin will send powwow information from his tribal office at Rt. 7, Box 21, Philadelphia, Ms 39350.

In October, 1987, Iron Eyes was made a lifetime member of the Native American Indian Association of Tennessee, which sponsors an annual fall festival and pow-

wow at Suggs Creek Saddle Club in Mt. Juliet, Tennessee, near Nashville.

There's a special reason why I treasure Mt. Juliet. It was there on October 18, 1987, in the midst of the great outdoor fall colors that Iron Eyes adopted me as his daughter.

We had had a private ceremony a year previously, and had been looking for the right place for the presentation to the tribes. Mt. Juliet and Sammy "Tonekei" White, for Master of Ceremonies, was the perfect combination for the special event.

Iron Eyes presented me with an eagle feather that had been blessed, a beaded ceremonial collar, and as a sign of family membership and lineage, an antique 1901 copper-cameo broach that his mother wore from 1901 to 1909.

He bestowed upon me a proud name "Oxshinnia," which in Cherokee means "You Are The One."

In turn I gave Iron Eyes gifts of food which are symbolic of life sustaining: pecans roasted in peanut oil, and for his sweet tooth, fresh honey, flavored by the finest of the soybean blossom, and peanut brittle, all of which came from my farm, my home, and my heart. The gifts served as a reminder that where I am, he will be welcome.

Tonekei was doing a great job reading the ceremony, which incidentally, I wrote and was approved by Iron Eyes. Most of my life Iron Eyes has been my good example. For seven years he has been my teacher, with serious study for the past two years. His approval was like receiving an A+ on a thesis for doctorate. The experience of working with him and studying under his supervision can't be measured in monetary value.

When a traditional Indian's heart becomes full, he cannot speak, thus the need for a master of ceremonies to do the talking.

Continuing with the ceremony, a short quote from the thoughts of Marietta in the voice of Tonekei:

"Marietta is honored to be chosen as the daughter of Iron Eyes Cody. She accepts her new name "Oxshinnia" with pride.

"To show her high esteem for him, Oxshinnia wishes her father to know how she feels about him. To her, he is as tall as the trees, as gentle as the spring rain, and in his heart is the warmth of the summer sun.

"She promises to listen to his words, to learn from him. She will teach others what he has taught her, so that all will know of her wise father."

Then Tonekei asked the singers for one song to make the adoption official and invited everybody to dance. Always the Head Man must be first and lead any dance. The drum made a sound. The bells on the ankles of Truman Ware, head man, jingled as he stepped into the arena. But he stood still. The drum sounded again as a request from Head Man for Iron Eyes and me to come and stand by his side, evenly with him, and dance. And that we did; the men with lively steps;

mine were calm and dignified. Head Lady Dancer, Dee Dee Goodeagle entered by my left side and others filed in afterward.

From the microphone came these words: "They're dancing! Good! Honoring Oxshinnia, new daughter of Iron Eyes!" Tonekei had thrown in some words of his own.

We danced once around the arena, then I led Iron Eyes out. Those who were already dancing continued another round. At this point, more dancers entered, hugged us, shook hands, and began to dance. President Donald Yahola (of NAIA) entered. This was when I noticed a dollar bill lying at my feet and picked it up.

By Indian custom, when someone is honored, that person must pay for any expenses that are incurred for the ceremony.

Iron Eyes third from left and Marietta in center, with five of the hundred dancers at the adoption. Head Man Dancer, Truman Ware is third from right.

In this case I was the honoree. If anyone so highly approves of the reason for the occasion that he gives a dollar to help with expenses, the ceremony is sanctioned. It's like a seal of approval and brings good luck.

When all the dancers had completed the circle, the head man, head lady, and master of ceremonies led them up facing us and every foot stopped on the last beat of the drum. More congratulations and another dollar was placed in my hand. It was Tonekei. Iron Eyes calls him "brother."

The ceremony was completed by calling twenty of our friends to come and receive a gift. Then I took several dozen beaded bracelets and string dolls that I had made and placed them on the ground out in mid-arena for all the children to come out and get. The kids swarmed me.

To commemorate the adoption, the following poem, a gift, was written by a Choctaw-Cherokee-Lumbee lady from Lennon, Michigan.

OXSHINNIA

By Jan Eden Creque

"You are the one"
    With heart so true.
I know for sure,
    For I know you.
Quiet dignity and grace,
    Not just painted on your face.
But in the heart and soul within.
    Content to struggle, dedication to win.
Belief in yourself, faith in God,
    Climbing hills where none have trod.
Seeing beauty where there's none,
    Happy in a job well done.
Out of confusion, making order,
    A well tended garden with flower
        border.
Hidden pain behind the eyes,
    Silent rain and sunny skies.
Strength that comes from gentleness,
    Love that's born of tenderness.
As running streams seek deepest water,
    You sought and found your Father's
        daughter.
Honor and love shine like the sun.
    In his heart and mine,
        "You are the one,
            Oxshinnia."

This Christmas smoke signal drifts to the Four Winds to proclaim a message from Iron Eyes and his adopted daughter, Marietta. Remake of a drawing by Clarence Ellsworth.

In Tennessee, 1988 has been designated "The Year Of The Indian." Many activities are being planned for the year. Information may be obtained from NAIA, 211 Union Street, Stahlman Building, Suite 717, Nashville, TN 37201.

Iron Eyes' parents were married at Red Clay, Tennessee; so be assured he will be around to help the state celebrate.

This world is blessed by the life of Iron Eyes Cody, who says, "Upon this earth, let us all lay down the lance of hate." What a great Indian father I have!

Among the Indians' most important weapons were the bows and arrows; with them, game could be killed at a distance with accuracy. When a likely piece of bow wood was found, it was taken home and saved for a later date. Arrowheads were made from anything that could be shaped or sharpened: stone, wood, horn, bone, copper, slate, shell, iron, etc.

Iron Eyes' effectiveness with bows and arrows led to his between-film traveling with Miller Brothers 101 Wild West Show, A. G. Barnes Circus, and Buck Jones Circus.

He toured with the Sidney Royal Agricultural Show in Australia in 1934. In research of the passenger list of the SS Monterey as of departure date September 24th, to Sidney and Melbourne, Australia, while looking under "C" for Cody, I could find no listing. I wondered if I had the wrong date; but when viewing the "I" section, there it was - IRON EYES, MR.

He made a name for himself, hunting bear and kangaroo with the bow and arrow, winning the 40-yard trophy from the Melbourne Centenary and the Coogee Archery Association.

It was during the Melbourne Centenary that Iron Eyes demonstrated his dancing in a command performance before the King and Queen of England.

There is no single Indian language. There are similarities in some tribes; but there are several hundred Indian tongues that are different from each other. Indian

languages have their share of gestures and grunts; but they are more involved than the simple "how" and "ugh" as is often heard in the motion pictures, especially the early westerns before our great Iron Eyes Cody could apply pressures for authenticity.

Indians often use one word so that it becomes a whole sentence; or they will have several words to describe the varieties of one thing. The correct word for "arrow" might depend on the use of that arrow: hunting arrow, or war arrow.

Sign language has been called the universal language. It began from the need to communicate among those who spoke so many different tongues.

Language has to do with the vocal

Teaching Jane Russell to shoot bow and arrow for movie, THE PALEFACE.

sound of words or combination of words; therefore, "communication by sign" might be a better term, but it is easier to say "sign language."

Today sign language is becoming a lost art, slowly passing away with the older Indian people who want so desperately to keep it alive.

Exactly who invented the system is not known. Traces of the use of sign language have been found all over; but it was among those who lived and moved in search of the buffalo that it became so proficiently used. The Plains Indians believed the Kiowas invented it. The Commanches say they learned it in Mexico. One thing is certain: there were at one time some five hundred tribes all needing to communicate.

Many signs are based on circumstance such as saying hello upon meeting someone, where are you from, why are you here? Then come the courtesies: come in, sit down, are you hungry, do you want to rest?

It does take some imagination to understand sign language, because some of it has been abbreviated, same as spoken language uses abbreviations. Changes occur when signs are being passed from teacher

Iron Eyes with Roy Rogers, making sign for two people who grew up together and are friends.

to pupil, according to the way the individual learns. Unless a person is highly skilled he might miss the meaning of a particular sign.

Silent communication allowed warriors to talk in battle; game could be sighted and indicated without sound; it assured complete attention be given to the one delivering the message; no looking away.

And lest we forget those wonderful smoke signals; this means carried messages over greater distances. A smoky fire was kindled and a blanket was waved above it so that the smoke came out in puffs. The spacing and number of puffs had various meanings.

Iron Eyes keeps sign language going and holds it high in the ways of tradition. His first book on sign language was used by the Boy Scouts of America who make sign talk a part of their curriculum and have helped to establish a continuing use.

We all use some sign talk when we hold a finger to our lips to signify silence, be quiet, don't say anything. We shake our heads from side to side to mean no; we nod to mean yes. We shake a fist to show anger; and for many years arm signals were used when driving to signal turning left, right, slowing or stopping. We wave a hand for saying bye. But these bits of usage are not enough to carry on a conversation.

Iron Eyes learned some sign language from his expert father as he toured with him in the wild west shows. Two of his father's friends: Buffalo Man, A Cheyenne; and Two Gun White Calf, A Blackfoot, spent much time keeping Iron Eyes out of mischief. They taught him enough so that he could talk to the different tribes as they moved about with the shows. Along the way, Iron Eyes met up with White Horse, a great Arapaho Chief who helped him improve his technique. Then through the efforts of his friend and great sign teacher, Colonel Tim McCoy, Iron Eyes rose to the height of proficiency as the skilled communicator he is today.

It is Iron Eyes' wish that the young people of today will care enough and find interest enough to keep sign language alive and teach it to their children so that the future generations will have it to use and enjoy.

Will Hutchins, studying HOW with author Iron Eyes.

Iron Eyes has authored five books: HOW, INDIAN SIGN TALK IN PICTURES (Boelter Classics 1952-53); LITTLE WHITE CHIEFTAN (Tenth Brand 1963); INDIAN TALK, HAND SIGNALS OF THE AMERICAN INDIANS (Naturegraph 1970); INDIAN LEGENDS (Noteworthy 1980); and IRON EYES, MY LIFE AS A HOLLYWOOD INDIAN (Everest House 1982).

HOW originally sold for one dollar, postage paid. Today the book is a collector's item, valued at fifty dollars. Yes, I have one among my treasures; and no, it's not for sale.

HOW has been used extensively by the Boy Scouts of America as their official study guide in sign language. The cover, drawings, and some of the photography was done by neighbor artist, Clarence Ellsworth, about whom the second book LITTLE WHITE CHIEFTAN was written.

LITTLE WHITE CHIEFTAN told the story of the life of Clarence Arthur Ellsworth. Each page contained a painting, drawing, or sculpture by Clarence.

Clarence loved the outdoor life. As often as his health, time, and money would allow, he traveled the country by means of self-made boats of any type. He spent days, weeks and months with the various Indian tribes, practicing his painting and photography.

Clarence and his drawings were accepted by the Indians in a manner in which no other white man could accomplish. He strove for truth in his work, keeping each tribe's customs and dress exact. There was no mixing of values for the sake of pleasing the white man with his sales.

The name "Little White Chieftain" was given to Clarence by the family of a beautiful Sioux Indian girl, the daughter of a chief. They had planned to be married; but she died before their wedding day. Clarence remained true to her by his continued artistry in his love of the Indian way of life.

Iron Eyes gave Clarence the lot next to his, on which to build a home. They shared a lifetime of friendship; they enjoyed making and hunting with bows and arrows, and photography. Clarence was the inventor of the mechanical means by which the camera shutter is simultaneously released with the flash, patent number 1220325. His biography was carried in 1959-61 WHO'S WHO IN AMERICAN ART. When Clarence died, his home was willed back to Iron Eyes.

The paintings and prints of paintings of Clarence Ellsworth are found in museums and private collections of Iron Eyes and others. Many enjoy his paintings that hang in the Southwest Museum in Los Angeles.

The third book, INDIAN TALK, is detailed on sign language and contains photos of the whole Cody family using the signs.

INDIAN LEGENDS contains stories of wisdom that Iron Eyes and Birdie learned as children; they are lessons to live by.

Statement by Iron Eyes:

"IRON EYES, MY LIFE AS A HOLLYWOOD INDIAN was a best seller; but I was unhappy with some of the contents. What I had told in truth only, somewhere down the line, was fictionalized for sensationalism without my knowledge. I am a traditional man and I had wanted that book to be honest; it wasn't. BUT IT

SOLD GOOD!"

An impressive honor was bestowed upon Iron Eyes in August, 1985, when he was made an Honorary Life Member of the American Buffalo Association, for his many accomplishments in the public sector and his friendship for the buffalo and those who seek to preserve its well being.

He was selected as the subject for the 1986 American Buffalo Journal. The painting by Douglas Weaver of La Mesa, CA was entitled: "PTA: A Brother, A Holy Spirit, A Way Of Life, Iron Eyes Cody." The word "PTA" refers to the generic Indian word for buffalo and the duel meaning for the spirit of the buffalo. Weaver's work was to commemorate the magnificent herds of buffalo of the past and the present day herds which will renew the link between man and buffalo, and to honor the Native American, Iron Eyes Cody. Weaver portrays Iron Eyes as the wise elder, communicating with the buffalo, by placing the head of Iron Eyes next to the head of the buffalo as though each in spirit knows the other.

A Limited Edition Lithograph of the painting was struck, five hundred museum quality on buckeye 100% rag, signed and numbered by the artist, priced at one hundred fifty dollars each. The money is divided between the American Buffalo Association and various Indian organizations selected by Iron Eyes. The size of the painting is 20x24 inches.

Litho #1 was presented by ABA as a gift to President Ronald Reagan, signed by both Douglas Weaver and Iron Eyes Cody.

For information on the lithograph, where to purchase buffalo meat, or how to obtain a buffalo cookbook, contact: The American Buffalo Association, Stockyard Station, Box 16660, Denver, Colorado 80216.

Most of us refer to the American Buffalo simply as "buffalo." Zoologists call it "bison." It has humped shoulders with a large head and neck, and fourteen pairs of ribs. The color ranges from brownish-black at the head to light brown at the rump. This wild animal somewhat resembles an ox, but has long, shaggy, coarse hair on the head, neck, and hump. The throat and chin has a beard. The horns are like those of cattle, only larger.

Some of the horns spread as wide as three feet. A bull might be twelve feet long, six feet high, and weigh 3,000 pounds. The female cow is smaller, about 900 pounds.

Buffalo mate at age three though they are not fully grown until age eight. They have been known to live up to forty years.

They have quick tempers, but are sociable within their herds. Bulls and cows graze together, eating mostly grass, small shrubs, and plants. A calf is usually born in May or June and is yellowish-red when born. The bull leader helps the cows defend the calves.

A society of young warriors who acted as leaders of a buffalo hunt were called Dog Soldiers. The hunt had to be controlled. If a single Indian rushed into the herd, he might get one or two buffalo, but he might scare the herd into a stampede and lose it. Dog soldiers policed the way the hunt was carried out. They were so strict on themselves in their high standards that if one was outnumbered in a fight, he singly stood his ground, knowing he would be killed unless others came to his rescue.

There were once great herds of buffalo in the area between the Appalachian Mountains east and the Rocky Mountains west. In the 1850's there were approximately twenty million of these animals; but by 1889, only thirty-nine years later, only five hundred fifty could be found. Many of the Plains Indians starved to death because the buffalo had been their main source of survival.

With the aid of a zoologist, William T. Hornaday who lived until 1937, game laws were passed to let the few remaining buffalo live and multiply. Now in the United States there are over one hundred buffalo ranches and approximately sixty thousand buffalo.

The buffalo was life itself to the Indian; it personified all that was necessary: food, clothing, and shelter. The whole animal was used. The meat was eaten, and the tongue was given as a delicacy to the chief. Hair was woven into cloth; jewelry was made from bones; teeth formed necklaces for the hunter; tendons made good sewing thread. The brain served as a tanning agent; the entrails were flasks for water and could be used as skin for drums. Scabbards were made from the tails. The chief wore the best buffalo horns so all would know he was the highest. Other horns were dipping utensils. Lucky was the Indian who had a buffalo skull to keep near his lodge so that good things in life would come to him.

The skull has highly respected spiritual value and is one of the main objects in the Sun Dance Ritual. To honor the buffalo in dance could bring good happenings because the buffalo would hear and return the honor.

As a small boy of ten, Iron Eyes

PTA: A Brother, A Holy Spirit, A Way of Life, Iron Eyes Cody. Painting by Artist/ Mystic Douglas Weaver.

Great hunter preparing hides.

acquired his first buffalo while accompanying his father in a wild west show near Lawton, Oklahoma. He fell asleep in the car and was awakened by the noise of a cow buffalo giving birth. The mother abandoned the newborn calf. Iron Eyes wrapped it in an Indian blanket, hid it until he got home, and plopped it into his bed, a big, fluffy feather bed to keep it warm, thus saving its life and making a close friend. It was raised with his dog. Iron Eyes, buffalo, and dog were inseparable.

The dog was named "Oh Boy" and every time Iron Eyes called the dog, the buffalo would come, too. Both answered to the name. Oh Boy Buffalo was tame enough to wear a harness and pull a sled. Iron Eyes proudly showed him at rodeos and fairs and gave buffalo rides in the shows. Tim McCoy asked him to parade Oh Boy Buffalo around in front of Grauman's Chinese Theater for city people to see.

Oh Boy Buffalo lived to be 42 years old. Even now when Iron Eyes sees a buffalo up close, he automatically compares it to the one he so well remembers from his childhood.

From the moment he saw the calf born and then abandoned, he felt immediate compassion for it and for all those that had been slaughtered nearly to the point of extinction. The feeling has remained throughout his lifetime. Currently Iron Eyes owns six buffalo on various ranches in California and Oklahoma.

The buffalo is coming back with an economic potential. Many states now have buffalo, and markets are carrying the meat. The buffalo may serve as a symbol of unity between the Indian and white man if we share in its preservation and enjoy its purpose.

A cowboy sings, "Oh, give me a home where the buffalo roam;" but it is the Indian who feels it so deeply within. Iron Eyes prays for the buffalo, remembering the life-giving strength it provided our

In WESTWARD HO THE WAGONS, 1956, with the buffalo that reminded Iron Eyes of Oh Boy.

ancestors. He is proud to be a member of both the American Buffalo Association and the National Buffalo Association.

The most important gift from the Indians to the white man was food. Life without potatoes and corn? I can't bear the thought. Thanks to the Indians who taught white settlers how to grow them, they are American staples, along with peppers, squash, peanuts, a variety of beans, etc. Whites learned from Indians how to cook, how to make tapioca, succotash, popcorn and hominy.

Have you ever wondered how hominy was made? As a child I watched many times as my mother made hominy in the big, black, cast iron wash pot in the backyard. My younger brothers and I carried the water and fire wood.

Wherever corn was raised, hominy could be made; it was an important food. Dry, shelled, field corn and wood ashes were boiled together until the hulls loosened. The hulls were removed with a ladle. The resulting grains were rinsed over and over again to remove any trace of the lye from the ashes. The corn was then boiled again, seasoned with salt and black pepper, and flavored with any meat bone, even one that had been boiled once already. I still enjoy hominy on a regular basis and will never forget learning how to make it many moons ago.

Indians used everything they could as a source of food. Tribes living close to water were grateful for the fish. They gathered maple sap as a sweetener, and salt when they could find some. They ate berries, roots, and wild plants. Wild rice was good with duck. Tea was boiled from wintergreen and sassafras. I've drunk gallons of sassafras tea, calling it root beer to the little brothers.

Foods could be boiled or roasted in ovens made by lining holes in the ground with hot stones. Meat was dried in the sun or smoked to preserve it.

Traditional Indian food was cooked in one container, for sake of space, time, and convenience. Nearly everything could be put into the stew or soup, giving the best flavor with herbs and spices.

In general, Indians ate one main meal per day, often in the middle of the morning. A family with food would share with others in the clan who had none.

In some states, laws have now been passed that change buffalo from wild game to commercial meat status and allow for state inspection of the meat. Therefore, more and more buffalo is being served in finer restaurants. It is more expensive per pound than beef; but the increased nutritional value outweighs the price difference.

Buffalo meat is tender and delicious (personal experience speaking). Several times I've been treated to a tasty buffalo burger, prepared by Chef Iron Eyes; and I always look forward to the next time.

We would like to share these Indian foods with you; but for now we'll just give the recipes. Back when great, great grandma was doing the cooking, measurements were by dab, dash, dollop, glob, pinch, smidgen, etc. She didn't trust those new fangled measuring cups and spoons; but for you modern day gourmets, the following are translated to reflect those "new fangled" devices of leveling.

Great chef at work!

108

BIRDIE CODY'S INDIAN MEAT PIE
(from my collection)

1 lb. ground beef	1 teas. salt
1/3 lb. sausage	1/4 teas. ground
1 large onion	cloves
1 stalk celery &	1/4 teas. nutmeg
leaves	1 teas. cinnamon

Crumple meats together. Put in kettle with about a cup of water with seasonings and chopped onion and celery. Cook for about half an hour. Pour into colander to drain. Put juices in ice box so grease can be lifted off easily.

Put ingredients from colander in a kettle. Add juice after removing top grease. You may have to add a little more water as we are now going to add about three medium diced potatoes to the mixture and cook until tender. Allow to cool. Taste to see if you need more salt. Mixture should be thick and not sloppy. Now make a thickening with some corn starch, arrowroot, or flour. Add and let cool.

Now make your favorite pie crust. Add cooled mixture to pie crust. Add top crust and bake for about an hour at 400 degrees.

Please remember this is the first time I have ever put the ingredients down on paper. I generally taste and taste to add more spices to bring it to the right taste as I remember it. Too much spice makes it bitter, so go easy until you get it just right. This pie is delicious hot or cold. ---Birdie

ARKANSAS FRESH CORN PUFFS

Scrape kernels and pulp from fresh corn, enough to make about 1½ cups of corn and milky pulp.

Begin to slowly heat three cups of oil in large cooking pot to temperature of 350 degrees.

Sift together ½ cup plain flour, 1 teas. baking powder, ½ teas. salt, ¼ teas. paprika (cayenne if you like it hotter), and ½ teas. black pepper. Mix in corn and three beaten eggs.

Drop by teaspoons into hot oil. Fry until light and golden. Drain. Makes about 3½ dozen.

IRON EYES' OLD-TIME INDIAN SOUP

1 pound lean beef (small chunks)	1 can hominy 16-oz.
1/2 pound fresh pork (small chunks)	1 can kidney beans 16-oz.
1 bay leaf	1 medium onion, chopped

Put all ingredients into cooking pot. Simmer slowly, the longer the better the flavor. Reduce liquid or add water as needed. Serves six people.

INDIAN PUDDING

1 quart milk	1 teas. ginger or
1/2 cup plain cornmeal	cinnamon
1/2 cup molasses	1 cup cold milk
1 teaspoon salt.	Cream (optional)

Heat quart of milk and stir in the cornmeal very slowly until it thickens. Remove from heat. Add molasses, salt, and spice. Pour mixture into a buttered baking dish. Pour one cup cold milk over it. Bake slowly at 275 degrees for two hours. During baking more milk may be added if so desired. May be served with or without cream.

WILD RABBIT WITH DUMPLINGS

Dress and cut up a three pound wild rabbit. Sprinkle with black pepper and dredge in flour. Heat 1/2 cup oil in cooking pot and brown rabbit on all sides. Drain. Pour off oil from pot.

Put rabbit back in pot. Add three pints water and simmer, covered, for two hours. Add 1/2 cup chopped onion, six medium carrots cut your way. Simmer another hour or until carrots are tender. Stir in three teaspoons salt.

To make dumplings, sift together 1 cup flour, 2 level teaspoons baking powder, 1/2 teaspoon salt. Combine 1 tablespoon oil with 1/2 cup milk and stir into flour mixture. Drop by teaspoon into boiling rabbit gravy. Cover and cook for five minutes. Serves four or five.

BUFFALO CHILI

Brown 2 large onions in oil. Add one and 1/2 pounds ground buffalo. Add salt pepper to taste.

Add:
Two 16-oz. cans kidney beans
Two 16-oz. cans tomatoes
Two tablespoons vinegar
Two tablespoons sugar

Simmer for 1/2 hour or until mixture is of thick consistency. Add chili powder to taste and cayenne pepper if you like it. Number it serves depends on how hungry you are.

BUFFALO BURGER PATTIES

3/4 lb. buffalo burger   1/4 cup milk
1 slice raw bacon,   1 egg
  cut fine   1 Tbs. flour
Garlic salt to taste   2 Tsps. lemon
Black pepper to taste   juice
1/2 cup cracker   1/4 Tsp. onion salt
  crumbs (rolled   2 Tbsps. melted butter
  fine)

Combine all ingredients. Mix well. Shape into patties. Broil or fry until brown. Makes six patties.

NOTES ABOUT BUFFALO MEAT

Leftover buffalo roast is great as sliced meat for sandwiches. Shredded roast makes good meat salad by adding mayonnaise and chopped onion.

Ground buffalo can be substituted for ground beef; it will be more lean and won't shrink. Compared to beef, buffalo has 1/2 the calories, 1/6 the fat, less than 1/2 the cholesterol, as well as one and 1/2 times the protein, and 1/3 more iron.

Biologically, buffalo do not marble (put fat in muscle); therefore, the meat is more lean, richer, and takes less to satisfy the appetite.

Buffalo are healthy because of the basic nature and biological attributes. They are raised without growth stimulants on grasses and natural grains.

The most acceptable taste is produced when cooked slowly at 250 degrees. Medium rare is more preferred than medium well done. It can become tough if cooked improperly, too fast, or at too high a temperature.

The taste buds of Iron Eyes have been tried and tested while judging many chili cooking contests. Drawings by John Steele.

SANDY'S FRY BREAD

BY Sandy Red Hawk, Apache

2 C. flour
3 tsp. baking powder
2 tsp. salt

2 T. sugar
3/4 C. milk
Corn oil

Combine and mix DRY ingredients. Add milk and mix until dough sticks together. Then cover with cloth and allow to sit about 30 minutes. Take dough and knead on floured board a few times (not too much); then pinch off 6 pieces. Shape into a ball and roll out in a round, approximately 1/8" thick (thicker, if desired). Heat oil in deep skillet and when hot, gently place dough in and brown on both sides. Drain on paper towel. Yields approximately 6 - 7" diameter breads.

Serve with refried beans, chopped onions, tomatoes, shredded cheese and lettuce on top for an Indian taco.

One of the most often asked questions at powwows and other gatherings is, "How do you make Indian Fry Bread?" We are pleased to include the recipe of Sandy Red Hawk. Page design and drawing by John Steele.

CHAPTER 7

DO INDIANS SMILE?

It is a common belief that Indians do not smile. I should say it's a common white man's belief, and especially thought by those who do not personally know an Indian. This notion probably comes from the Indian custom of not showing emotion in public.

An Indian might not shed tears at the death of a loved one; but inside his heart breaks. "Poker-faced" is the term used in describing the look presented in public. Even laughter can be suppressed if practiced; and small children learn it from their parents. The silence and stone-faced look is a matter of custom, a way of showing politeness by spending a period of time in massive silence.

When a stranger or friend came to an Indian's lodge, there might have been a short greeting such as, "You have walked a long distance." Then, the guest would have replied, "Yes, a long distance." Then there would be a motion to sit down, and food would be offered. Later, after a rest in silence, maybe a pipe would be lit and passed to the guest. Then some easy conversation would begin. The better a guest was known, the more relaxed they would become. Storytelling could go on for hours as the guest related the details of his travels. His woes or funny mishaps would delight his hosts.

Also as of custom, in some tribes the individuals could barely speak to each other when the relationship was one of extreme respectfulness. This did not mean coldness, but rather it was the strong nature of their mutual feelilngs.

There is an old story that many years ago a delegation of Indians, as a treat, were taken to a stage show, a musical, on a trip to Washington, D.C. They loved the entertainment. As they sat in the dark theater, their dignity and reserve melted to such a relaxed point that their whoops of joy nearly stopped the show.

Most Indians maintain a kidding relationship with their clan, but the Muskhogean tribes required a man to avoid his mother-in-law and a woman to avoid her father-in-law. Otherwise, they were expected to itch all over. The power of suggestion was strong; if one expected to itch, he would itch. Medicine Man would have his hands full!

I have found that Indians have a great sense of humor. One time I handed Iron Eyes a free ticket. "Oh, a free ticket," he said. Then he read it: "This is a FREE TICKET. It's not good for anything. It's just free." We had a good laugh.

For Iron Eyes' birthday I gave him a small, nicely wrapped box with a cute little bow on top. Good things come in small packages! By the time he had it opened, I was already laughing. He looked at me out of one eye as he held it up between two fingers. "One sock," he said, "What in the world am I supposed to do with one sock?" "I wanted to have a two-day party," I replied, "and tomorrow you'll have another present." Later I handed him the second sock, and inside it was his birthday gift.

We both believe that laughter is the best medicine in the healing of emotional wounds. It helps when a person can look at all phases of his life and not take it so seriously. If you have no one else nearby to smile at, look in a mirror and smile at yourself. If you have nothing more to give to comfort the needy or afflicted, just offer a smile and a prayer. You'll like yourself better for it.

. . .

As proof that Indians do smile, please carefully examine the following pages in the manner of Raymond Burr (Perry Mason); then you be the judge, and accept your own decision.

I rest my case. DEFINITE PROOF INDIANS DO SMILE. Victor French and Iron Eyes, 1986.

Iron Eyes with Sorrell Booke and Denver Pyle (Dukes of Hazzard, TV). Photo by Clint Brown.

Iron Eyes with Charlton Heston and Rod Redwing, 1958

Iron Eyes with Mike Mazurki, 1983

Iron Eyes and Clayton Moore, 1982

Iron Eyes with Ted Knight and Ray Bolger, 1979

Iron Eyes with Peter Graves

Iron Eyes with four Rose Parade princesses, 1985

Looks like a smile to me. Iron Eyes and
U. S. Senator Jennings Randolph. Photo by
Ankers Capitol Photographers.

Iron Eyes with Lana Turner, 1981

Iron Eyes with Snuff Garrett and Roy Rogers, 1980

Iron Eyes with Charles Starrett (The Durango Kid)

Iron Eyes with Yul Brenner and Lynn Wood, 1983

118

Iron Eyes with Chuck Connors

Iron Eyes with Phyllis Diller who says: "Never go to bed mad. Stay up and fight."

Iron Eyes with Johnny Grant and Jack Klugman. Photo by John Maxon.

Iron Eyes with Mr. and Mrs. Robby Benson, 1983

Iron Eyes and Dinah Shore, 1977

Iron Eyes with Loretta Lynn

120

Iron Eyes and Jerry Colona, 1974, at Motion Picture Country Home

Iron Eyes with Jane Wyman

From left: Iron Eyes, Ray Bolger, Pat O'Brien and Scott Brady, 1979

Iron Eyes with Phil Harris

Iron Eyes with Sunset Carson and Royal Dano

Iron Eyes with Mary Dorr, Roy Rogers and Dale Evans, 1987

Iron Eyes between Jack Benny and Mary Benny

Iron Eyes with Billy Grammar and Roy Acuff

Robert Altman with Iron Eyes, 1981. Photo by Lisa Law.

123

Iron Eyes with Ben Johnson, Eddie Dean and Monte Hale, 1975

Iron Eyes with Jackie Coogan and Monte Hale, 1980

Iron Eyes with Victor and Mary Buck

CHAPTER 8

NATIONALLY FAMOUS RELATIVE

Ralph Emery on the TV show NASH-VILLE NOW asked Iron Eyes the same question that has been asked so many times before, "Did you pose for the Indian Head Nickel?" Iron Eyes answered, "I'm not that old."

One of the Indians who did pose for the nickel in 1912 was Big Tree, Birdie Cody's great uncle. From the five Indians

Iron Eyes at age 11, with Big Tree

Yowlachie and Big Tree

considered, three were selected. From the three, Big Tree was chosen for profile.

James Earle Fraser designed the nickel, known as the Buffalo, Bison, or Indian Head Nickel. Its first issue was in 1913.

The buffalo on the reverse side was modeled after Black Diamond, in the New York Zoological Gardens. There were two varieties of the coin: the first showed the bison standing on a mound; the second had the bison on a thin straight line. That first year over 38 million of the nickels were minted. Seldom is one found in circulation today.

According to some historians, Big Tree (Isaac Johnny Johnson) was born in 1875. The six-foot, two-inch Seneca began his movie career in minor roles in 1915.

He usually won the role of "Chief" because he carried himself tall and proud with the look of strength and nobility. He died July 5, 1967, on the Onandanga Reservation in New York. To Iron Eyes' knowledge, he died at age 101, being nine years older than was told to the public.

His over one hundred films included: THE FRONTIERSMAN (1927), SIOUX BLOOD (1929), RED FORK RANGE (1931), LAST OF THE MOHICANS (1932), THE SINGING VAGABOND (1935), HILLS OF OLD WYOMING (1937), THE GIRL OF THE GOLDEN WEST (1938), STAGECOACH, DESTRY RIDES AGAIN, DRUMS ALONG THE MOHAWK (1939), BRIGHAM YOUNG (1940), WESTERN UNION (1941), SHE WORE A YELLOW RIBBON (1949), and DEVIL'S DOORWAY (1950).

An Indian Head Nickel is embedded in the concrete on the front porch of Iron Eyes' home as a way of paying everlasting tribute to Uncle Big Tree.

The famous Indian head nickel profile of Chief John Big Tree was later adopted as the insignia of the Pontiac Division of General Motors.

Big Tree was the model for the statue "End of the Trail"

CHAPTER 9

YOWLACHIE'S FUNERAL

Eagle Feather having flesh pierced by Iron Eyes at Yowlachie's funeral

When Chief Yowlachie died in 1968, it was Sioux Medicine Man, Eagle Feather who notified Iron Eyes that Yowlachie had requested an old-fashioned Indian funeral.

Iron Eyes planned the service at Pierce Brothers' Mortuary in Los Angeles, and dressed the Yakima Chief in his best regalia, complete with a war bonnet.

The eulogy was presented by Iron Eyes. Among those who stood up and said nice things about Yowlachie were the members of the Westerners Corral, the International Club of Historians.

As the ceremony began, an eagle feather was placed in the Chief's hand for safe guidance to the Happy Hunting Ground. Flesh was cut from the arms of Eagle Feather whose eyes were tightly closed but obliging as Iron Eyes performed the ritual. Bits of flesh were placed in an earthen cup inside the coffin. Eagle Feather rubbed blood on Yowlachie's face and ceremonial paints on the body. With blood on his hands, Iron Eyes called upon

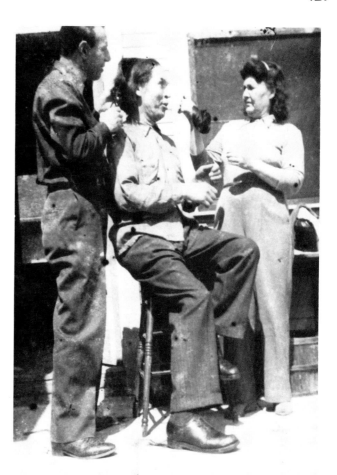

One of many good memories – Iron Eyes trying to give Yowlachie a hair cut according to direction of Mrs. Yowlachie

Smart Injuns traded good ponies for this? From left: Silvermoon Cody, cranking car; Big Tree, Yowlachie, and Iron Eyes. Shooting Star is behind the wheel. Circa 1935.

The Great Spirit and extended the Calumet, Peace Pipe to the Four Winds. The smell flavored sweet grass drifted through the room. Earth was sprinkled on the quieted Yowlachie to symbolize the return to dust.

In the background, drums were beating as Robert Cody played the funeral song on the Indian flute.

Yowlachie, the famous Yakima Indian singer for the Metropolitan Opera before he turned actor, lay there looking like he was just sleeping through the whole thing. Says Iron Eyes, "We really gave him a good send-off, just the way he wanted it."

CHAPTER 10

RESPECT TO A GREAT AMERICAN

1987 photo by Lamar Gilbert

When a traditional Indian man is honored, his heart becomes full, and he cannot speak. Someone close to him who knows his thoughts must speak for him. I do so speak.

Indians are a proud people; they cannot be domineered. Yet, when we look at this great man, Iron Eyes Cody, his face creates in us a feeling of reverence and humility. Silently he commands respect from the nation, and he receives it. When he offers The Great Spirit Prayer, we listen with our hearts and applaud the one who gives it.

Iron Eyes is a conservative, caring man, keeping only enough money for his basic needs and sharing the rest with those less fortunate. He endeavors to help the dignity of his people and of all people. He loves; he never hates. He is the best of two worlds: the Indians and the white man; he draws them together in unity.

Iron Eyes teaches the power of positive thinking in all walks of life. He feels that education should be the goal of each individual person, and that we should join together and learn from each other.

If you want to hear a fabulous story, listen to Iron Eyes. He can spin endless yarns, but they are true stories. If you ask him a question, don't expect a quick answer; he'll get to it in his own way and in his own time; and along the way you will be the recipient of a fascinating lesson in life. Listen to him and learn.

The only true native of America is the American Indian. I met this one a long time ago and I knew immediately that we share a common heritage. He was someone whom I admired and respected and characterized myself as following in his footsteps (though I'd be a mighty tired somebody to follow this man's footsteps). Iron Eyes never stops. I wonder if he ever sleeps; maybe he sleeps standing up. Anyway, he has affected my lifestyle and influenced what I believe are the better traits I possess. Anyone who has ever crossed paths with Iron Eyes will know what I mean. He leaves a lasting impression on our lives.

Everything Iron Eyes stands for is readily visible in his face, his movement, his actions, his voice, and his life. He reflects all that's good, right, and worthwhile. He lives and breathes for the betterment of mankind.

There is a swiftness in this man of untiring energy. There is much yet to be done; and each day he does as much as he can for as many as he can.

If you peak from behind a tree and see Iron Eyes in your neck of the woods, count yourself lucky, for this is a busy, busy man. He is either coming from or going to one charity benefit or another.

Iron Eyes is a true hero: modest, humble, and gracious. When he passes your way, take a moment to enrich your life by just looking at him, if nothing else; or speak to him and hear his voice. You'll always remember and wish you had had more time to spend with this great man.

This kind and gentle man's love reaches the four corners of the earth and surrounds the whole world. Iron Eyes' concern for all living creatures is evident in his caring for animals and the natural habitat. He thanks The Great Spirit daily for his good existence and this good earth. He prays for those close to his heart.

Iron Eyes stands up for those things that make and keep America great. He is a friend. Birds fly from the trees and feed from his hand. I can't imagine the loss to this country had there not been the man with the tear.

A famous man named Sitting Bull once said, "Let us put our minds together and see what kind of life we can make for our children." I want to thank you, Father Iron Eyes, for all you are teaching me of my Indian heritage. I shall forever treasure your Peace Medal. I make my own personal treaty with you to work to help preserve all that which is good and valuable to mankind.

On the following pages are words of praise from some of Iron Eyes' friends. They honor him also. If some "roast him a bit," remember that he loves a great sense of humor.

To quote Will Rogers, "Get someone else to blow your horn and the sound will go twice as far." Well, Iron Eyes Cody, hang on. We are about to toot your horn!

-----Marietta

130

Iron Eyes Cody and daughter, Marietta Thompson.   1987 photo by Lamar Gilbert, Knoxville, Tennessee.

I will treasure forever the blessed feather that Iron Eyes sent me - both for what it stands for and that it was from Iron Eyes, my buddy and dear friend. I have never heard him say an unkind word about anybody in my life. He doesn't drink or smoke. You'll never meet a better person or a nicer person than Iron Eyes Cody. Iron Eyes and I were in three movies together: CHARGE AT FEATHER RIVER, CUSTER'S LAST STAND, and THEY DIED WITH THEIR BOOTS ON.

---Bill "Little Horse" Barbour
Alexander, Arkansas

They say Columbus discovered America in 1492; Iron Eyes says it never was lost in the first place. Iron Eyes, if they try to give it back to you, unless they return it in its original condition, don't take it.

---Pat Buttram

Iron Eyes Cody, there's only one "America" and you are all of it.

---Bill Robinson, Vice President
Native American Indian Association
of Tennessee

From one "American" to another - we will be brothers when The Great Spirit calls us to hunt the buffalo in the faraway place.

---Donald Yahola, President
Native American Indian Association
of Tennessee

Iron Eyes, I've killed you a lot of times and you've killed me a lot of times. Isn't it amazing we're both still living?

---Terry Frost

To Iron Eyes Cody, a great American Indian, a good friend who always helps when he can. It's a pleasure and privilege to know you.

---Marion Callahan
Mrs. Terry Frost

The one thing about Iron Eyes that sticks in my memory is his rendition of The Great Spirit Prayer. It is beautiful and so is Iron Eyes.

---Archie Campbell
Nashville, Tennessee

Iron Eyes, you will never know how much you contributed to the success of our 10th Angel Awards ceremony. We are so grateful to you for the time and energy spent in our behalf. We wish the greatest continued success for you in every endeavor of your life.

---Mary Dorr, Founder/Producer
Angel Awards, Los Angeles, California

Iron Eyes, we all love you. One of the great treasures I have is the eagle feather you presented to me. I'll always treasure it. I wouldn't even throw a gum wrapper on the ground.

---Eddie Dean

1987 photo by Melanie Smith

Iron Eyes Cody's presentation at our last meeting convinced this writer that one person can make a difference in what is often seen as a cruel and unfair world. He can be proud of his accomplishments in the areas of environmental protection, helping handicapped kids, and working for the betterment of his fellow Native Americans, to name a few.

---Tom McGowan, Program Chairman
Gasco Retirees Association

Iron Eyes, thank you for your unexpected help at the Crash Corrigan Days in Simi Valley. Hope to see you at some of the upcoming events, and if not, you are always a welcome guest if you ever find time to come to the Iverson Movie Location Ranch.

---Bob Sherman,
Sherway Publishing Company
Chatsworth, California

1987 photo by Azzam Abdulwahab

Iron Eyes, you have honored us with your gracious presence, and I trust that the filming will serve not only the needs of the mission to be better known, but also to help Americans be more aware of the needs of the First Americans, especially the children. God bless you and all you do for children of all races, and especially the ones we are serving. His peace and joy in abundance, In Him.

---Father Tom Westhoven, SCJ
St. Joseph Indian School
Chamberlain, South Dakota

Iron Eyes, our thanks for allowing Tisja and Tanja to ride with your group in the Rose Parade. Your thoughtfulness in talking with the girls before the parade made them really feel a part of the group. Please accept my family's appreciation for allowing my daughters to express their pride in our Indian heritage by riding with someone whom we consider an "exceptional" American Indian and a friend.

---Mel Twist, TeePee Engineering
Riverside, California

Iron Eyes, my son Robby will be receiving his Eagle Scout Award. This will probably be one of the proudest days of my life, and I have you to thank for encouraging him to join five years ago! I remembered how honored I was when you gave me one of your eagle feathers when we were together at the Duke Children's Classic. It is now one of my prized possessions.

---Cliff Snider
(promoter of the Iron Eyes Cody
National Environmental Stamp)

Iron Eyes, on behalf of the Academy of Television Arts and Sciences, thank you very much for attending the 17th Annual Allen Ludden Memorial Party at Rancho Los Amigos Medical Center. Your participation was greatly appreciated. The patients loved it, and will do better in the coming months because of it. Thank you for sharing your time, your love, and your "self." Your being there made a difference.

---Betty White
Honorary Chairperson

Photo by Bill Ames

Iron Eyes, on behalf of the Coca-Cola Company, the Greers Ferry Lake and Little Red River Association, the Keep Arkansas Beautiful Association, the U.S. Army Corps of Engineers and myself, thank you so very much for honoring us with your presence and participation in the 17th Annual Greers Ferry Lake and Little Red River Cleanup. It was such a pleasure and joy to have you with us. You made this occasion most enjoyable for a lot of people and you made a great number of friends. Friends who think and believe as we do in Keeping America Beautiful and preserving the good life in Arkansas, the natural way.

The Cleanup was the most successful to date. Twenty-six hundred volunteers cleaned 300 miles of shoreline, 25 miles of river and 40 miles of roadsides. Five thousand plus attended the Fish Fry and Entertainment, consumed 1,500 pounds of catfish and enjoyed nine groups of entertainers and Iron Eyes Cody. In fact, all the weekend events were most pleasant and enjoyed by all. Your Great Spirit Prayer was inspiring and moving. You touched all of us, and we will always remember this occasion. Good luck on your new book. We look forward to learning the true story of Iron Eyes.

    ---Carl Garner, Department of the Army
       Little Rock District
       Corps of Engineers
       Heber Springs, Arkansas

Iron Eyes, thank you for being our 1985 Western Walk of Fame Honoree. We love you and are so proud of you and what you have done.

    ---Joanne Darcy, Public Relations Director
       Western Walk of Fame

Iron Eyes, since you were here filming the TREASURE Forest spot, thousands of people in Alabama are recognizing the significance of woodland management through the airing of your message. Hope to see you again.

    ---Cynthia K. Page
       Alabama Forestry Commission
       Montgomery, Alabama

Iron Eyes, everyone at Window Rock is still talking about the visit of the famous Iron Eyes Cody to the Navajo Police Department. We appreciate very much your coming to the reservation to assist the Navajo Police in honoring their heroes. Your presence at the ceremony was a major factor in making it a great success. You are a great friend and an inspiration to all people.

    ---John Philip Clark, Jr., Chairman
       Navajo Police Awards Committee
       Window Rock, Navajo Nation, Arizona

Iron Eyes, thanks for joining me on the Ground Breaking and helping kick off our facility for the Spastic Children's Foundation. We hope to do a tournament again next year and celebrate the completion of the facility and our young people moving in. Thanks for making my stay at the Knoxville Film Festival so easy. Keep up the good work. Always your friend.

    ---Ben Johnson

1987 Photo by Dean Norman

Iron Eyes, your participation in the "Day of the Mocassins" in Upland and the "Unknown Indian Award" in Los Angeles as well as appearing in Mayor Bradley's office, impressed the non-Indian people as to the significance of all three events. The youngsters who received the certificates of participation from you will long remember the day. Young Billy Klubb who received the autographed SIGN LANGUAGE is now a celebrity among his peers at the Foothill Knolls Elementary School.

---Jack C. Fletcher, Coordinator
Preservation of the Unknown Indian
Upland, California

Iron Eyes, I want to personally thank you for your generous donations to the museum. The bronze sculpture by Ken Ball is an excellent likeness as is the John Steele painting. The calumet, pipe bag, and paintings of John Fire are of special interest to our Indian collections.

---Joanne B. Hale
Executive Director and Vice President
Gene Autry Western Heritage Museum

Iron Eyes, thanks so much for the great honor you bestowed on me at Sycamore Park on National Indian Day! It truly is gratifying to be able to serve on the Board of Directors of the Little Big Horn Association.

---Dr. William V. Malcolm, Jr.
Arcadia, California

Iron Eyes, I'm sure the fans lining the parade route expressed it better and more enthusiastically than I'm able to, but I still want you to know how much I appreciate your participation in the Hollywood Christmas Parade.

---Johnny Grant, Vice President
Public Affairs/Special Projects

When the first atom bomb was exploded and the mushroom-shaped smoke ascended upward, Iron Eyes saw it and said, "I wish I had said that." There's a fallacy about Indians that they never laugh. Indians have the greatest sense of humor with their children. Iron Eyes, just look at the way your mother dresses you funny. And you cry a lot; but you're my brother and I love you.

---Jock O'Mahoney (blood brother)

Iron Eyes, we are extremely proud of the Pomona Valley Writers' Association's first book ever - EXPRESSIONS OF THE SOUL. This little book was made possible because of you and the generous time you gave our organization at our celebrity fund raisers. We will forever be grateful and treasure you as an Honorary Member of the Association.

---Patricia Ann Almazan, President
Pomona Valley Writers' Association
Ontario, California

Iron Eyes, I wish to thank you on behalf of Durango Boot and all our employees for your support in advertising our product. The thing I find most heartwarming is your continued support of your people and their children. This is the American Way... but unfortunately, many of us forget to help our fellow man. What a pleasure to know a person of traditions.

---Pete Hillier, President
Durango Boot
Franklin, Tennessee

Iron Eyes, I would like to thank you for showing the picture I made of the group on The Nashville Palace on the WTBS Nice People Program. That pleased me more than words can express.

---Howard Moore
Sumter, South Carolina

CHAPTER 11

WHAT NEXT?

A hot air balloon ride. At Heber Springs, Arkansas. 1987 photo by Marietta.

After 200 movies, hundreds of radio and TV shows, commercials, advertisements, thousands of personal appearances at fund raisers and powwows, does Iron Eyes still have goals? Oh, yes!

There are plans in the making for sequels to the movies GRAYEAGLE and EL CONDOR. A new one, SHADOWS IN THE HIGH SIERRAS with Clint Walker and Neil Summers, is a possibility. Disney continues to utilize a great deal of Iron Eyes' talent and time.

Honorary Chief, Honorary Mayor, Honorary Sheriff, Iron Eyes has been filmed, collected, roasted, toasted, stamped

In spaceship with Jerry Elliott. Friend Jerry is Osage engineer at Houston Space Center.

In cockpit of 737. Photo by Captain Karl Gruber, 1986.

and approved. What lies ahead? Maybe a trip to the moon! He has already been fitted with a spaceship as revealed in photo from Houston (Texas) Space Center. Good luck, Dear Friend; may The Great Spirit be with you always.

And as Iron Eyes says when something is finished -

WELL, THAT'S IT!

138

SELECTED BIBLIOGRAPHY

Adams, Les, and Buck Rainey. SHOOT-EM UPS. New York: Arlington House, 1978.

James, George Wharton. WHAT THE WHITE RACE MAY LEARN FROM THE INDIAN.
    Chicago: Forbes & Company, 1908.

McCoy, Tim, with Ronald McCoy. TIM McCOY REMEMBERS THE WEST. New York:
    Doubleday & Company, 1977.

Parker, Arthur C. SKUNNY WUNDY AND OTHER INDIAN TALES. New York: George
    H. Doran Company, 1926.

Pitts, Michael R. WESTERN MOVIES, A TV and Video Guide to 4200 Genre Films.
    North Carolina: McFarland & Company, Inc. 1986.

Steiger, Brad. MEDICINE POWER, The American Indian's Revival of His Spiritual
    Heritage and Its Relevance for Modern Man. New York: Doubleday & Company,
    1974.

1987 photo by Norman T. Foster

INDEX

142